SOCIAL SERVICE DELIVERY
A Structural Approach to Social Work Practice

SOCIAL SERVICE DELIVERY
A Structural Approach to Social Work
Practice

Ruth R. Middleman and Gale Goldberg

COLUMBIA UNIVERSITY PRESS
New York and London

Library of Congress Cataloging in Publication Data

Middleman, Ruth R.
  Social service delivery: a structural approach to social work practice.

  Includes bibliographical references.
  1. Social service. 2. Social workers. I. Goldberg, Gale, joint
author. II. Title.
HV40.M517   361   74-3304
ISBN 0-231-03730-9

Preface

The reader may well wonder how a book can be written by two people. Certainly all who collaborate must find some way of working the problem out, and there are no guidelines that help one know how to do this in advance. Our own experience in collaboration did not begin with this manuscript. We have collaborated in planning and teaching courses and have had the excruciating experience of writing one paper almost line by line jointly. At times during that experience we came to understand how it was possible that Gilbert and Sullivan were not on speaking terms. For the pulls and tugs of idea, preference, and style can sabotage even the most congenial partnership. If this book seems coordinated and smooth, it is due to hours of discussion, to occasional bursts of inspiration appreciated by the other, to periods of waiting and nonproductivity, and to the watchful eye of John D. Moore, Associate Executive Editor at Columbia University Press.

The reader must know, however, that the total credit for the theoretical formulation, the quadrant conceptualization to describe social work practice as well as the practice principles comprising the structural model, belongs to Gale Goldberg. In other words, the discussion set forth in Chapters 2, 3, and 4 are exclusively hers. It seems especially important to emphasize this fact at the outset since the reader might be misled to surmise that the first author, Ruth Middleman, deserves any of the credit for this innovation.

Middleman appreciated Goldberg's theoretical leap despite the fact that such a reconceptualization of social work practice threatened some of the previously cherished faith and dogma familiar to those who have taught social work practice in the past. We spent many exciting hours debating the rewards and costs associated with abandoning certain widely sanctioned ideas about practice in favor of a different approach and we decided to move ahead. This was followed by a series of dialogues (soft and loud) through which we fleshed out and further refined the new practice we were going to teach.

Our freedom to create and teach something wholly new was a matter of circumstance. Unlike many of our colleagues in social work education who think new and exciting thoughts that die in the curriculum committee, we were not saddled with organizational tradition, tenured colleagues with huge investments in the past, a well-stocked library, and previously established relations with social agencies. The graduate department of the School of Social Administration at Temple University was brand new. This was enough encouragement for us to seize the initiative.

There were people whose reaction to our work was most reassuring. In particular, Scott Briar's thoughtful responses urged us ahead. Ann Hartman, Gordon Hearn, and Joseph Vigilante were also encouraging.

The enthusiasm of our students and their ability to put these ideas to work helped us increase our clarity and devise teaching approaches that would convey the ideas to others in an orderly way. At the technical level we received valuable help from Mrs. Diane Simpson, our research assistant, from Mrs. Barbara Brockelhurst, our typist, and from Mrs. Dorothy M. Swart, our copy editor.

R.R.M.
G.G.
Temple University

Contents

SOCIAL SERVICE DELIVERY
A Structural Approach to Social Work Practice

The man who wears the shoe knows best that it pinches and where it pinches, even if the expert shoemaker is the best judge of how the trouble is to be remedied.

John Dewey

Chapter 1

Introduction

The term "service delivery" reflects a central concern in American life—economics. Production, distribution, exchange, and consumption occupy at least half the time of those in the mainstream, while concern with the pressures that result from noninvolvement or limited involvement in the economy occupies far more than half the time of those who are out of the mainstream. A consumer psychology orders our view of life.

THE AGE OF THE CONSUMER

Businessmen have learned that the world does not beat a path to the door of the man who builds a better mousetrap. They know that the key elements determining a product's usage include what it looks like, how many people know it exists, who else has one, and how widely it is distributed. Hence, they invest heavily in package design, advertising, and distribution mechanisms. And as the consumers become more aware of the power that inheres in their role—the power to use or avoid a given item—as they become more sophisticated about the products offered for their consumption, they seek more control over what goods are to be produced and sold.

It is no accident that services are coming to be viewed in the same way. That is to say, with respect to potential consumption, quality is only one measure of a service—necessary, but not sufficient. The nature of the service, its goal, its distribution, and its delivery are equal, if not more significant determinants of consumption. And as consumers of social, educational, and health services become more aware of their power and more sophisticated about the services offered to them, they seek to influence not only what services are offered, but how they are offered, where they are offered, and who offers them. The drive for community control of schools, social agencies, and hospitals, the increased frequency with which the words *parity* and *equality* are heard, represent discontent with power differentials. Clearly, more people want more of a say in what happens to them.

Consumers are making the point with increased stridency that "human" services are not human, that they are ill-conceived, that they are palliative fragments designed by those with biased frames of reference who lack sufficient knowledge about the users, and that history reveals their failure. Consumers are questioning the nature and form of services; they are questioning the arrogance of the providers; and they are questioning the professionals' competence. These "Who says so?" questions attack doctors' control over health systems, teachers' control over parents in educational systems, and social workers' control over clients in social service systems.

The economic-political exigencies of the times pit whole segments of the population against each other. The man in the street, the politician, and the provider of services blame each other and/or the populations in need, for it is simply incomprehensible to find and attack the more abstract common enemy—a system of economic arrangements that has produced an industrial technology far out of line with the social arrangements needed to live with it. Like the broom of the sorcerer's apprentice, the economic system takes on a life of its own and sweeps furiously with ever-increasing momentum, while the system of social services, which is expected to provide a comfortable life, desperately hangs on, ill-attended, underfinanced, and viewed at the moment as a wasteful, burdensome investment. The political system is more responsive to the vested interests of the economically powerful than to the interests of the poor. If interests were to be represented equally, the poor would have about fifty congressmen and thirteen senators to represent them.[1]

Against the backdrop of increasing recognition that existing social arrangements are inadequate, that differentials in access to means systematically keep the poor and other powerless groups from attaining their goals, and that these "voiceless" segments of the population will no longer settle for palliatives and promises, the posture of the social worker has begun to shift. For some time now, the literature of the profession has directed the social worker toward greater participation in politics, to use his clout where it counts in matters affecting social legislation, hence social conditions. The literature has directed social workers to advocate for clients' entitlements and to support client movement into the political arena. But there is a "how-to-do-it" gap between injunction and action, particularly at the microlevel.

MICROLEVEL PRACTICE

The term "microlevel" refers to a view of man in society in which the unit of attention is the plight of individuals, in contrast to the term "macrolevel," which views man in society from the perspective of general problems such as poverty and delinquency. This book describes a new microlevel practice model consistent with the emerging social welfare-through-social-change philosophy.

The book was written for the social worker who questions the systematic inequities surrounding the disbursement of society's resources, who wants to "hang in there" with the powerless, angry client because of an ethical commitment to how it ought to be. It was also written for the supervisors and administrators, the planners of social programs, the developers of social policy, and the researchers who devise the measuring instruments that assess the effectiveness of a practice or a program; for persons in roles aimed to support and make room for the basic services will do so more effectively to the extent that the various approaches to direct practice are described and opened to public scrutiny. It was not written for the social worker who wants to be a therapist, for it offers no guidelines for people changing except, perhaps, at a collegial level.

The book furthers the continued interest of social workers in matters of social justice, particularly their interest in how unjust social conditions are experienced by individuals in their everyday lives, and how a difference can be made. It describes, and illustrates with examples of workers in action, the ways in which the social worker can respond to clients and their social distress, as these clients come with their needs to the social agency, or as they are encountered in present-day urban industrial life, in the public schools, the mental health centers, by parole boards, in housing projects and boarding homes, mental hospitals, institutions for the aged. This book is for the microlevel practitioner, whether supervisor or worker, whether with an MSW or a BSW, who wants to assume a social worker orientation rather than a method-based orientation, who wants to deliver services through a social work methodology equally applicable in a one-to-one, group, or community context. That is, the book is directed to the social worker who wants to work

with the client wherever he is met and be free to pursue
what needs to be done according to the tasks worked out
together.

CONSUMERISM AND SOCIAL PROBLEMS

The enlightenment of the consumer is a positive force that
the social worker can connect with toward the reduction of
social distress for all. To accept the notion that social worker
and client alike are consumers, joined to each other as fellow
strugglers through the vast bureaucratic mechanisms that control their everyday lives (with the specialized know-how for
negotiating and surviving the morass sometimes possessed by
social worker, sometimes by client, sometimes by neither) is
to adopt a new perspective for their work together.[2] Some social workers might wish to fight and try to explain away the
client's anger, frustration, and disappointment with the services he has had. Some social workers might suffer pangs of
exasperation (and self-doubt) with client "ingratitude" for
their well-intended ethical and moral commitment to serving
others as a helping person. But these reactions help no one.
It behooves the social worker to "get with" the client in a new
way, to be for him even in his anger.

This will be a different, possibly an uncomfortable position
for the social worker. For his expertise may be identified by
the client as having been used to maintain the social arrangements planned by some "elite" in behalf of others. And the
client is right. All too often the social worker has served as
society's gatekeeper of the *status quo* rather than as an informed
strategist who offers a special know-how to help clients change
their social situations. The social worker no longer has the
monopoly on being the conscience of society.[3] Others have
taken over this role who can be even more effective. The social
worker no longer needs to interpret the needs of the poor to
those who control the resources, for the poor can do it them-

selves and they do not want him to speak for them. But social workers can, if they work hard enough, lend their special knowledge where it counts. Through an assertive posture, they can bring to bear their specialized knowledge and skills to help others in their quest for the material and personal resources that make for social well-being.

The general awakening of the public to the social condition of man, the alarm at the accelerating pace of economic forces that threaten to engulf all—the discontent is shared by those who have "made it," by those who now see that they are outside it and demand full-fledged membership in society, and by those struggling at some midpoint within the system. Just as consumers protest the devastation of the physical environment by the business-industrial complex and force some perhaps costly response, so can consumers protest the neglect of the social environment that spawns even greater social problems for tomorrow's world and force the costly investments that must be made for human survival. For the increased public dissatisfaction with the precariousness of today's life is now part of the consciousness regardless of attempts to redefine who should bear the financial cost of meeting human needs. More people know that the promises of the Constitution have been more rhetoric than reality, that domestic tranquillity has not been insured, that the general welfare has not been promoted, and that the other basic rights enumerated for individuals have not been assured for all.

It is all too apparent that the myth of America as a nation of equals, a classless society, is an ideal that has never been energetically pursued. And now more segments of the population are aware of their powerlessness and are objecting to the political, economic, and social inequalities of the times. The poor, the blue-collar worker, and the white-collar worker alike —each from his own vantage point—feels the crush of the ever-increasing pressures of an economic system which consign him

to increasingly insignificant slots as the bureaucracies and cor-
porations grow bigger. And with a level of affluence visibly
increased for some and a greater awareness that there is economic and technological potential that could be deployed more
to social and human needs, the expectations for a better life and
the impatience with present conditions make the mission of
social work, as a part of this struggle, ever more urgent.

A STRUCTURAL APPROACH

In contrast to other orientations to practice that may aim to
help individuals adjust to their situations, to understand their
motivations, to gain insight, or to change their ways of thinking and acting, the structural approach aims to adjust the environment to the needs of the individuals. The basic assumptions underlying this orientation are elaborated in Chapter 3.
Because the orientation differs, the practice principles, the
guidelines for practice, also differ from those presented in other
texts. These new principles are explained and illustrated in
Chapter 4. Chapter 5 describes four major roles that the struc-
turally oriented social worker performs at different times. Chapters 6 through 10 focus on skill, and define and illustrate specific
behavior through which the practice principles are applied in
action. In Chapter 11 organizational forces are reviewed, and
some of the problems impinging upon the social worker in social welfare bureaucracies are explored. Chapter 12 presents a
new way to think about social science and social work practice.
Finally, in Chapter 13 we consider the charges that social work
practice has not been effective and reflect upon what we have
tried to specify in this book, as well as our ongoing focus for
practice and research in the future. In the Appendix the reader
will find one detailed report of service in which the specific behaviors that the worker uses are labeled.

The reader will find connections between some of the ideas presented here and those of earlier social workers who held similar interests and concerns about their world. We are not the first to suggest, for example, that:

. . . social and economic conditions and the intellectual and political spirit of the times exert profound influences upon the particular . . . problems which concern us and upon the forms of help which develop and flourish.[4]

Others have pointed this out with respect to social services [5] as well as education.[6] Neither were we the first to note that two modes of social service helping have derived from the *Zeitgeist* of the times, popular according to the particular values and view of man that flourished with the times. For it is well-documented that

situational modes of help, demanding as they do the questioning of the social environment and change in the social environment, will flourish during periods of political or social reform . . . periods of "acute social change." . . . Intra-psychic modes of help will be prominent during periods of political or social conservatism.[7]

More than fifty years ago Mary Richmond saw the need for a social work practice that emphasized more than casework and wrote:

. . . social casework would be only a fragment if separated from the much larger field occupied by social work in general . . . family case workers [should] study and develop their work at its point of intersection with social research, with group activities and with social reform or mass betterment.[8]

Our notion that the social worker should aim to "work himself out of a job" has its counterpart in Wooton's contention that social work should be "self-liquidating." [9] And emphasis upon more than the intrapsychic phenomena was pointed to by Charlotte Towle:

that families live in streets amongst neighbors, not in a vacuum, that much of most lives is spent in factories or other work places, and that people are affected by what happens outside their homes as well as by their domestic relationships.[10]

Towle also proclaimed loud and clear to the workers in the 1940s: "The social caseworker has labored all too long in futile attempts at helping the individual feel better on an empty stomach." [11]

It was Bertha Reynolds who long ago told school social workers:

The contribution of social casework is to supplement the best public administration, not to struggle to make up for the mistakes of a poor one. If a faulty school curriculum is causing every year thousands of school failures, it would be stupid to engage visiting teachers to work individually with the unsuccessful children. Why not change the curriculum and do away with that particular problem at one stroke? [12]

This has been reemphasized more recently as a directive applicable to the needed thrust of social workers in the field of public education.[13] Another injunction, compatible with ideas that will be encountered here but coming from a different perspective, is that

social workers should concentrate on being the social expert, mastering and interpreting the complex rules and requirements of the intricate bureaucracies dispensing services to the public and initiating appropriate action when necessary rather than pose as miniature psychiatrists.[14]

Other discussions of problem formulation and interventive

responses will be mentioned in subsequent chapters with references to related sources.

The major focus will be on present practice rather than on history. Throughout social work's brief history, practice has been conceptualized differently from time to time. Perhaps this stems from social work's view of itself as essentially a *responding* profession. Social workers have responded throughout history to what the times seemed to demand according to the knowledge and tools they had available. Unlike the scientists and engineers of the space industry who held a public sanction to create the times, social work held a societal mandate mainly to deal with the times. Social workers have been trouble shooters for an imperfect set of social arrangements, often equipped with blank cartridges that made more noise than impact.

But more than ever, many social workers want a hand in designing and creating the times. They want to initiate; not merely to respond. They do not wish to remain agents of social control, no matter how humane, for they do not want to perpetuate an inadequate *status quo*. This book aims to translate these more general social change imperatives into specific principles that can guide the practitioner as to what moves he will (or will not) make with specific sufferers.

BASIC ASSUMPTIONS

Two central assumptions are inherent in the approach:

1. Individuals' problems are not viewed as individual pathology, but as a manifestation of social disorganization.[15] Thus, the clients of social services are not categorically seen as impaired or deficient individuals, a different breed from the rest of society. Rather their life circumstances may be more precarious, more restrictive, more crushing than those of other populations.

2. The response of the social work profession to the need for social change is the obligation of the social worker wherever he

is in the bureaucratic hierarchy. In fact, it *begins* with how the
direct service deliverer conceptualizes his response to a specific
sufferer. Social change is not separated from social work, not
relegated to specialists within the social work profession (community organizers, planners, social policy-makers); rather, it is
pursued at every level of assignment, every working day by all
social workers, and especially by those who must face the clients
directly.

Part 1

The Structural Approach

Chapter 2

A Frame of Reference for Social Work Practice

The relatively short history of social work has been characterized more by diversity than by unity. Practices have differed in accord with different fields of practice (medical social work vs. psychiatric social work vs. child welfare work), different methods (casework vs. group work vs. community organization), different schools of thought (functional vs. diagnostic vs. problem-solving), and even different purposes (rehabilitation vs. socialization vs. resocialization vs. education vs. social action). A caseworker from the diagnostic school employed by a mental health agency concerned with rehabilitation engages in activities quite different from those of a group worker from the functional school employed by a child welfare agency concerned with socialization. While the former's work has been known to look like therapy (and the worker officially titled "therapist"), the latter's activities are frequently mistaken, by laymen and other social workers alike, for recreation. And what, if anything, is there about these diverse practices that makes them social work?

That this apparent lack of professional identity has drawn concern from various quarters is evidenced in the many individual and committee attempts to find the "generic," to find some underlying something that bridges the diversity and attests to the fact that there is a single social work profession. To date, the similarities that have emerged are largely in values, and while this may be sufficient to ameliorate our own identity crisis, it is hardly sufficient for our clients who rarely know what to expect from any of us.

If a profession *is* what it *does,* that is, if it is defined by its actions, then we must look to the activities of the social work practitioners for the data from which to define our boundaries. For while values attest to a measure of similarity, they are abstract and intangible and serve *only* to include. A more concrete definition by which activities can be classified either as "social work" or "not social work" is needed, for the counterpart of identity is repudiation.

To describe a need is obviously easier than to prescribe a way to meet the need. Nevertheless, it seems possible, at least in a gross way, to locate much of what is currently done in the name of social work along two bipolar dimensions. These two dimensions, locus of concern and person(s) engaged, describe four categories of activity to bound the profession conceptually (see Fig. 1).

TWO DIMENSIONS

"Locus of concern" constitutes the rationale for social work intervention. The poles on this dimension are: (1) the plight of John G., a specific person suffering in relation to particular facets of various problems (for example, a man who cannot get a job because he is a Chicano and cannot get decent housing because he is poor); and (2) the plight of all John G.'s, a general category of persons identified as sufferers by definition of a social problem (the poor, minority groups).

"Person(s) engaged" refers to those people with whom the

Figure 1

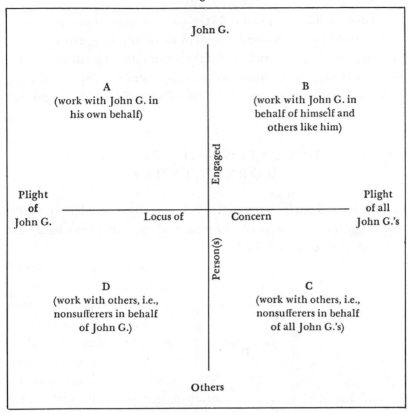

social worker works at various times in accord with his rationale for intervention. The poles on this dimension are: (1) John G.; and (2) others. On the one hand, the social worker may engage individuals and/or families and/or community groups in helping themselves and each other to change the particular situations that limit their functioning and exacerbate their suffering. Or the social worker may engage others (neighbors, congressmen, local merchants, other professionals such as teachers, lawyers and/or nurses) in helping an individual, family, or group of clients. Congressmen, for example, may be engaged by the social worker to amend housing laws that pro-

tect landlords but not tenants. Local civic leaders may be mobilized to demand additional day care centers, more accessible
health services, an improved system of monitoring employment
practices in local branches of large business organizations. Or
neighbors may be enlisted to provide specific supports during
a particularly trying time in the life of an individual or a family.

FOUR CATEGORIES OF SOCIAL
WORK ACTIVITY

The four categories of social work activity bounded by these
two coordinates (locus of concern and person(s) engaged) are
labeled A, B, C, and D in Fig. 1.

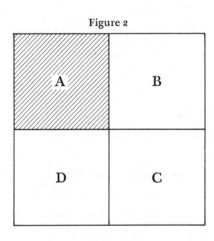

Figure 2

Quadrant A designates all
activity in which the social
worker directly engages John
G., out of concern with his
particular plight. To illustrate, one worker at a community mental health center
found isolation and loneliness to be the major recurrent themes expressed by her
clients (the plight of specific
persons). To help alleviate
this problem, the worker directly engaged the clients in
forming a telephone network through which they communicated
with each other every day. That is, John $G._1$ called John $G._2$ who
called John $G._3$. John $G._3$ called John $G._4$ who then called John
$G._1$. (See Chapter 4 for a description of the process.) The creation
of such a self-help network comprised of, and for the sole benefit
of, the few, specific people engaged is typical of activity in Quadrant A. A-type activity also includes work with families on

problems various members are having with each other, and work with individuals who are having problems with themselves.

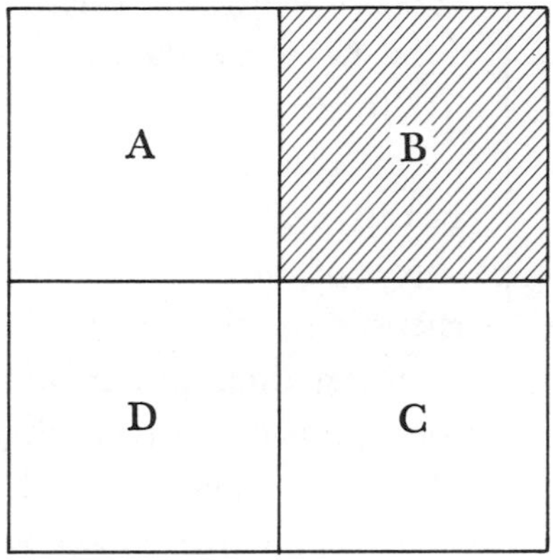

Quadrant B designates all activity in which the social worker directly engages John G. (a specific sufferer) out of concern with the plight of all John G.'s (a category of sufferers). Typical activities include working with some tenants (specific sufferers) to press for home improvements for all tenants (a category of sufferers), and working with a committee of senior citizens to plan programs for a larger senior citizen population. In other words, the typical Quadrant B activity involves direct engagement of one or a few specific people for the benefit of themselves and others like them.

Figure 3

A	B
D	C

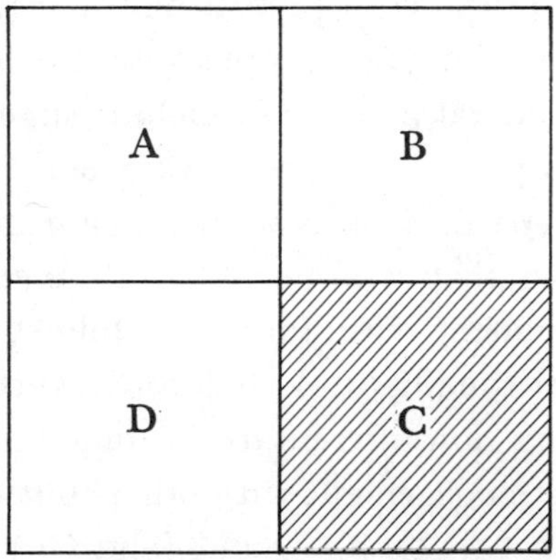

Quadrant C designates all activity in which the social worker directly engages others (nonsufferers) out of concern with all John G.'s (a category of sufferers). Examples include research, social policy development and analysis, social planning, fund raising, lobbying, and organizing scattered programmatic efforts to manage or alleviate a particular social problem into coordinated units for comprehensive social service delivery.

Figure 4

A	B
D	C

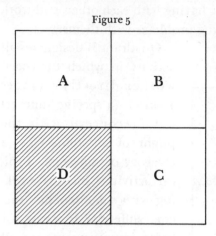

Figure 5

A

B

D

C

Quadrant D designates all activity in which the social worker directly engages others (nonsufferers) out of concern with the plight of John G. (a specific sufferer). To illustrate, another worker at a community mental health center learned that some of her clients were spending a whole day in line awaiting their prescriptions for tranquilizers (the plight of specific persons), while other sufferers were on a long waiting list, unable to get prescriptions at all. The situation was largely a result of the limited number of staff psychiatrists. In an effort to deal with the problem, the worker sought to organize general practitioners in the community (nonsufferers) to take on the prescription-writing function for persons in their neighborhood who needed the psychotropic drugs.

Had the worker organized some of those people who had to stand in line (the sufferers) for purposes of pressuring the mental health center to hire more psychiatrists or pressuring the local physicians to extend their general practice to include supervision of persons on psychotropic drugs, the worker activity would have been classified as type B. That is to say, organizing some sufferers to do something that will benefit both themselves and others (direct engagement with John $G._1$, John $G._2$ and John $G._3$ out of concern for the plight of all John G.'s) is a B-type activity, while organizing nonsufferers to do something that will benefit sufferers (direct engagement with others out of concern with the plight of John $G._1$, John $G._2$ and John $G._3$) is a D-type activity.

Other D-type activities include supervision, consultation, staff training and development, and administration.

RESEARCH VALUE

In addition to providing a classificatory scheme for ordering thoughts about social work practice, the four-quadrant model has some potential for guiding research. For example, it can be used to track the activities of a given social worker at work in a particular instance, or to compare his activities across instances, thus providing a mechanism for determining the typical activity of a particular worker in different problematic situations. Holding the type of situation constant, it is possible to track the activities of different workers in order to determine typical social worker activity in that kind of situation. So too, holding the type of situation constant, differential social worker activity as a function of: (1) school of thought; (2) field of practice; and (3) methodology can be examined. In such ways as this, we can collect data that will tell us what social workers do irrespective of differences in orientation and setting for practice (common activities), and what social workers do as a function of their different orientations and practice contexts (differential activities).

BEYOND RESEARCH

What social workers do may be quite different from what social workers ought to do. Research can contribute to knowledge of the former, and it can provide evidence to substantiate or disclaim the existence-in-action of a single, unified social work profession. But research cannot tell us what social workers ought to do.[1] When the data are in we will have to decide

whether we like all of it, part of it, or none of it, and that deci
sion will be made quite independent of the data itself.

Nevertheless, the frame of reference and the information collected and organized can focus our attention on possible gaps
in the range of approaches to social service delivery. And recognition of gaps can serve as a springboard for redetermining
specializations and for developing new approaches to serving
the heretofore unserved segments of the population frequently
labeled "unreachable" as if, somehow, our own limited repertoire of intervention strategies were their fault.

Chapter 3

Assumptions, Assignment, and Areas of Specialization

Definition of the cause of a problem is a potent force in determining action to solve it, for that limits the range of alternatives from which a solution can be chosen. For example, if the cause of unemployment is defined as lack of motivation, then efforts to deal with the problem will be directed toward motivating the unemployed. On the other hand, if the unemployment is explained as a breakdown in the structure of opportunity, then efforts to solve the problem will take a very different direction.

While it is obviously ridiculous to define a psychological problem such as fear of heights in social terms (e.g., buildings are too tall), the tendency to define social problems in psychological terms is a subtler version of the same mistake. And it is just such a fallacy of the latter type that has made some social workers unwitting parties to the mounting conspiracy against the poor.

The tendency to define social problems in psychological terms is closely related to the concept of the inadequate man on which such goals as increased ego strength are based. "Inadequacy" is a relative term. It refers to a disparity between the skills and resources of a given man and the demands of a given situation. If it is believed that the man ought to be more skillful and/or resourceful, more able to meet the demands of the situation, then the man will be labeled "inadequate." If, on the other hand, it is believed that the situation ought to place fewer demands on the man, ought to be more responsive to the needs of the man, then the *situation* will be labeled "inadequate." Thus, to say that a given man is inadequate is at one and the same time both a description of disparity between that man and a particular situation, and a value judgment attributing blame for that disparity.

The practice model suggested here presupposes that large segments of the population—the poor, the aged, the minority groups—are neither the cause of, nor the appropriate locus for, change efforts aimed at lessening the problems they are facing. This is not to deny that some people do, at times, engage in self-defeating behavior. The point is that inadequate social arrangements are predominantly responsible for many of the situations that are frequently defined as products of those who suffer from them.[1] Poverty, for example, was not created by the poor. Nor was racism invented by the blacks. And attempts to change individuals instead of the social exigencies that mitigate against them perpetuate the existence of such problems.

PROFESSIONAL ASSIGNMENT

The assumption that inadequate social arrangements are predominantly responsible for the plight of many clients of social agencies suggests the need for social workers who can help people to modify the social situations that limit their functioning. In response to this need, the following professional assignment is proposed: The social worker should help people to connect with needed resources, negotiate problematic situations, and change existing social structures where these limit human functioning and exacerbate human suffering.

This professional assignment is presumed to hold across agency settings. In other words, the service delivered by a social worker is conceptualized as a professional social work service rather than the service of a particular agency. Much as an obstetrician delivers babies, and delivers them in the same way irrespective of what hospital employs him, the social worker should perform the same professional assignment irrespective of his employing agency. In both instances, the service that the professional renders is the service of his profession.

Agencies define client populations and provide resources, but they do not determine the functions of the professionals they employ. This is not to deny that the way in which a worker implements his professional assignment must be modified in accord with the organizational restrictions of different agencies. The point is that the basic thrust does not change, although the specific movements of the worker may need to change.

Fulfillment of the professional assignment specified here demands performance of all four types of work defined by the Quadrant Model in Chapter 2. This is a tall order for any single social worker to carry out. Moreover, while the worker is involved in C-type activities (research, social policy development), what happens to the persons he left behind in Quadrant A? For example, who will help Robert Hernandez to get a job while the social worker is engaged with congressmen, local businessmen, and government agencies about putting into operation policies that guarantee equal employment opportunity for all? Conversely, who will work toward alleviating the common plight of minority groups through changing discriminatory employment practices while the social worker is busy helping Robert Hernandez to get a job? For pragmatic reasons at least, some division of labor is necessary.

SPECIALIZATION

Social work practice has always been divided in some way. But the specializations were not designated *a priori* in accord with definitive knowledge or a hypothetical construct of the whole. Rather, specializations evolved in the course of actual work, and partial theories to justify them appeared later.

One problem posed by evolutionary development, as opposed to *a priori* designation of specializations, is that of determining the amount and kind of additional specializations that are required. In other words, how will we know when we have arrived at the whole? Perhaps this partially accounts for social work's reluctance either to completely embrace or completely reject any innovation in practice. With no over-all, orienting scheme, with no image of what the whole should look like, there is no basis for separating the relevant from the irrelevant.

Related to this is the problem of recognizing gaps in social work practice. The absence of a scheme that organizes and gives meaning to the various specializations suggests that each is a whole unto itself, and that the profession is a loose federation of functionally autonomous units. How can there be gaps when social work is so conceived? If there is a whole of social work practice with an assigned or an assumed social function to perform, then specializations must be seen as parts in relation to other parts, each deriving its special responsibilities from, and having meaning only in relation to, the whole.

It should be noted that social work practice does not fall "naturally" into any particular set of subunits as opposed to any other particular set of subunits. Practice specializations must be arbitrarily defined, and in this sense, any scheme for partitioning the whole is as logical as any other scheme. The important issue is that there be some scheme, some theoretical construct (albeit tentative) that represents the whole and specifies the relationship among parts, irrespective of the particular way in which that whole is partitioned.

The four-quadrant model is one way to conceptualize the whole of social work practice. It guides our discussion of practice here, and serves as a point of origin for dividing social work practice into the two complementary areas of specialization diagramed in Fig. 6. Since specialization was necessary for pragmatic reasons, so too the overlap in Quadrants B and D are necessary for pragmatic reasons. The overlap is intended to prevent built-in gaps that hound theorists, confound practitioners, and frustrate clients.

Figure 6

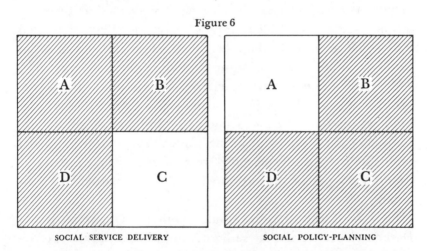

SOCIAL SERVICE DELIVERY   SOCIAL POLICY-PLANNING

Quadrants A, B, and D can be used to describe the practice of social work in the area of social service delivery, while Quadrants C, B, and D can be used to describe the practice of social work in the area of social policy planning. Since Quadrant A is presumably specific to social service delivery, and Quadrant C is presumably specific to social policy planning, Quadrants A and C could be considered the exclusive categories of activity that provide the needed division of labor. With respect to the example cited earlier, the social worker in social service delivery could then help Robert Hernandez to get a job, while the social worker in social policy planning could work on policies to assure equal employment opportunity for all.

Since both practice specializations would operate in Quadrants B and D, these could be considered the mutual categories of activity that provide the overlap to control for gaps between areas of specialization.

Given the above, it seems reasonable to assume that every instance of social work in social service delivery would begin in Quadrant A, with the expressed needs of a particular person, and extend to Quadrants B and/or D in accord with the demands of the client task. "Client task" is defined as the deleterious aspect of a problem impinging on the client, translated into a change goal. On the other hand, every instance of social work in social policy planning would begin in Quadrant C and extend to Quadrants B and/or D in accord with the demands of the social task. The "social task" is defined as a social problem translated into a change goal.[2] In other words, the objectives of social policy planning would grow out of the social problem itself, while the objectives of social service delivery would grow out of the expressed needs of a particular client system.

Since both specializations would operate in Quadrants B and D, their respective activities might, at times, look alike. In terms of Quadrant B, for example, either specialist may organize a group of tenants to press for improved maintenance and repairs for themselves and others living in the same housing project. As the specialists proceed from different loci of concern, however, their work manifests certain important differences.

The social worker in social policy planning may organize tenant councils in various housing projects in an effort to bring about broader social change with respect to tenants' rights. His concern is with a category of sufferers (the residents in public housing projects) rather than with any single instance within that category (the plight of John G.$_1$, John G.$_2$, John G.$_3$, and others in the Glenloch Housing Project). Thus his organizing job is not finished when any one tenants' council is organized, but his work with those particular tenants is finished. The worker moves on to organize other councils in other housing projects.

The social worker in social service delivery, on the other hand, organizes a group of tenants in response to their expressed need for improved maintenance. The worker's concern is with the plight of these particular tenants. When this group of tenants, with the worker, has accomplished the task (the manager has arranged for necessary repairs and improved maintenance), the worker is out of the tenant-organizing business. He may still be involved with these particular tenants in any number of other problematic situations, however (prejudicial attitudes of teachers in the local school toward the children of these tenants, inadequate public welfare grants).[3]

To specify a professional assignment and designate areas of specialization in terms of activity provides an orientation to practice, but it does not define practice itself. In other words, such a formulation, while essential to a coherent, systematic practice, is too abstract to guide intervention. Elaboration of a practice requires specification of a set of principles, operational definitions of the principles, the functional roles that derive from those operationally defined principles, and the explicit acts which the worker should perform in order to implement his professional assignment in accord with the operational definitions of those principles.

Chapter 4

Basic Principles of a Structural Approach to Practice

Every instance of social work involves an intervention into the relationship between people and their social environment in order to improve the quality of that relationship. The ultimate target of change may be the people, the social environment, or the relationship itself. The accumulated body of recorded experience in social work includes a variety of conceptual models to guide people-changing [1] and relationship-changing.[2] In the structural model described here, the social environment is the primary target of change. The social worker intervenes to improve the quality of the relationship between people and their social environment by bringing to bear, changing, or creating social structures.

The structural model rests on four basic principles:

1. The worker should be accountable to the client(s).

2. The worker should follow the demands of the client task.

3. The worker should maximize the potential supports in the client's(s') environment.

4. The worker should proceed from an assumption of least contest.

The Principle of Accountability to the Client(s). This

translates the basic assumption of "adequate man vs. inadequate social arrangements" into action. People suffering in relation to their social situations are presumed competent to describe the pressures upon them and to explain their need. Therefore, social work practice takes, as its starting point, the task confronting a particular client or set of clients as it is expressed in terms of their felt need. In other words, the pressures on the client(s) define the task, and the task is always to lessen those pressures. This task, explicitly understood by worker and client alike, constitutes one of two essential parts of the service contract.

The service contract operationalizes the principle of worker accountability to the client. A service contract may be said to exist when both worker and client explicitly understand and agree upon the task to be accomplished and what the worker will do to help accomplish it. This contract is not a written document, as a literal interpretation of the word would suggest. Rather, the term is used metaphorically to indicate that worker and client have verbally agreed upon what will be done and how it will be done. The service contract is a working agreement.

The client, with the help of the worker, describes the pressures on him (job discrimination, poor housing), and these pressures, in turn, define the task to be accomplished, what must be done to alleviate the pressures which the client describes. In the instance of poor housing conditions, for example, the task may be that of obtaining necessary repairs or obtaining a different house, depending upon the preference of the client. In the event that all possible efforts of worker and client do not accomplish the client's preferred task, they may jointly agree to work on an alternative task. Or, if there is no alternative acceptable to the client, the contract may be terminated.

When a task acceptable to both client and worker has been

determined, the worker defines the way in which he will help
the client to accomplish it. Should the worker's definition of
his share be unacceptable to the client, either the worker or
the client may suggest an alternative way for the worker to
help. If worker and client cannot agree on what the worker's
part should be, then no contract can be made. Should worker
and client agree, then the contract is established.

As changes in the definition of the task may occur as the
work proceeds, so the definition of what the worker will do may
also change. This change may be necessitated by changes in
the task, or by the implications of additional information obtained in the course of working on the original contract. In
any event, changes in the contract must be discussed and agreed
upon before action continues.

The extent to which the terms of the service contract are
specified in detail is less important than the social worker's intent to be completely open. That is, the worker should not have
goals or methods that he keeps secret from the clients. The mandate to establish a contract with each client or set of clients requires the worker to state his intentions explicitly. This not
only insures the client's right to decide whether or not the
worker's intended behavior is acceptable, but it also insures the
worker's awareness of what he is about.

Because the contract openly specifies what worker and client
have agreed upon as the task to be accomplished and the
worker's part in helping to accomplish it, at least theoretically,
the client is able to hold the worker to that task and the part
they both agreed that the worker would play. That is, the
client can hold the worker accountable for his actions. While it
is recognized that clients who feel (because they frequently
are) powerless are unlikely to confront a worker who may be
subverting the terms of the service contract, recognition of
their right to do so sets a different tone for the worker-client
relationship.

Social work by contractual arrangement has advantages such as reducing the relative powerlessness of the client in a helping relationship. Rather than being a dependent recipient of worker behavior beyond his control, the client is a partner in determining, every step of the way, what will be done and how it will be done. And the client is not called upon to trust blindly a person he hardly knows in order to get help.

In sum, the principle of accountability to the client translates the basic assumption of "adequate man" into action through the structural mechanism, the service contract, comprised by the task which is defined by the pressures on the client and the part the worker will play in helping to accomplish that task.

The following episode illustrates the accountability principle.

One of the fifth-grade teachers stopped me in the hall to tell me that a girl in his class was having problems with one of the other children. He asked me if I would talk with her, and I said that I would. A short while later Debby came into my office and sat down without saying anything. I waited several moments and then said, "I was talking with Mr. Taylor a little while ago and he seemed concerned that you were having some problems with some of the other kids in the class." I paused and waited to see if Debby would say anything. When she didn't, I asked her if *she* thought that there was any problem.

The social worker presumes that Debby is competent to describe the pressures on her. She does not act according to the teacher's perception that Debby has a problem, for it is quite possible that what may seem like a problem to the teacher may not be felt as a problem by Debby. And even if Debby does consider it a problem, she has a right to refuse the social worker's offer. But Debby does feel some pressure, and with the help of the worker she begins to describe her situation.

Debby then replied that the other kids have been teasing her, and that she has been upset. I said that teasing could make you feel pretty bad. She nodded.

I asked her if she'd like me to help her talk to the kids that tease her. She said that it seemed like a good idea, but from the look on her face, I could tell that something was bothering her. I said, "You don't look as though you think it's a good idea."

The worker picks up a nonverbal clue that Debby is not really in agreement with her suggestion, and she does not violate the intent of the contract by accepting Debby's verbal "yes" when her facial expression seems to indicate "no." Rather, the worker questions the double message that Debby is communicating. In response to the worker's acknowledgment of her hesitancy, Debby begins to describe a feared consequence.

Debby hesitated and then said that she was afraid the other kids might start a fight with her afterward. I told Debby that I had not thought of that and agreed that it could be a problem. I said that I guessed that could be really upsetting and pointed out that if she really wanted to get together with the kids who tease her, this could be one of the risks she would have to take. I asked Debby if she understood what I was saying, and she said that she did.

The social worker does not try to convince Debby to take action. Rather, she confirms that such a consequence is possible and encourages Debby to consider whether talking with the children who tease her is worth the risk. The choice belongs to Debby, for the consequences of the choice are hers to bear.

Debby decides to wait until the children tease her again, and a service contract is established.

Debby was silent for a few moments and then said that she didn't want to do anything until the children started to tease her again. She said that when they did, she would tell me. I asked her if she wanted me to wait until I heard from her again and at that time she would tell me if she wanted me to help her talk to the kids. She said yes, and I agreed to her plan.

The terms of the contract between Debby and the social worker were openly specified and agreed upon by both parties. No action would be taken unless another incident arose and Debby indicated to the social worker that she wanted her help. Hence Debby possessed the power to determine the direction of the worker-client relationship, if in fact she wanted to continue it at all.

The Principle of Following the Demands of the Client Task. This principle requires the social worker to move from quadrant to quadrant. For example, the worker may help a Puerto Rican child suffering from racism at school to talk with his teacher about it (Quadrant A). In addition, he may engage the faculty and administration in creating an atmosphere more congenial to the needs of Puerto Rican children (Quadrant D). Or, if necessary, he may organize the parents of Puerto Rican children at that school to confront teachers and administrators (Quadrant B).

Prerequisite to B-type activity is the identification of others suffering in the same situation. If the worker is to include B-type activities among his alternatives, he must consistently and systematically look beyond his client to see if there are others facing the same task. For example, B-type activity is not a viable alternative when only one Puerto Rican family is suffering the effects of racism at the local school. When other Puerto Rican families are also victims of racism at that school, however, the need for structural change rather than an individualized plan which results from a case-by-case approach is more evident, and B-type activity (social action) becomes an alternative for accomplishing the desired change. The demand that the worker consistently look beyond his client to see if others are suffer-

ing in relation to the same phenomenon translates the essence
of a structural approach to social work—meeting social needs
through social change—into actual practice behavior.

As the worker moves from quadrant to quadrant in pursuit of
the client task, he engages both the client and others, in different configurations, at different times. That is to say, A-type
activity may be carried on with an individual, with a family,
or with a group. Similarly in Quadrant D, the worker may engage one community person or a group of community people in
behalf of client interest. And in Quadrant B, the worker may
engage an individual, a family, or a group in behalf of themselves and others suffering from the same pressures. In other
words, the worker not only moves from quadrant to quadrant
in accord with the demands of the client task, but he also
engages different configurations of people as the work demands.

For example, when the worker agrees to help three residents of a public housing project to get needed home repairs,
his client is this three-person group with the common task of
obtaining the repairs. In the course of working on this task the
worker may engage the local representative of the city housing
authority (D-type activity with an individual), or he may engage the housing authority representative along with representatives from related agencies (D-type activity with a group)
in an effort to obtain the repairs.

Following the demands of the client task also implies the
need for role flexibility. That is, the worker needs to use different sets of behaviors at different times, depending upon the
nature of the task and of the situation at any given point.

Four recognizable sets of behaviors can be subsumed under
the role names: (1) broker; (2) mediator; (3) advocate; and
(4) conferee. The role of broker is perhaps the most familiar
one. The social broker stands at the interface between client
need and social resources, helping the former to connect with
the latter. But social brokerage is not enough; for clients and

agencies do not always recognize their complementarity of interest, that each needs the other in order to survive. As a result, needed service may not be rendered. In the role of mediator, the social worker tries to help client and agency to recognize their complementarity of interest and to act accordingly.

But complementarity of interest between client and agency is often more apparent than real. Many agencies have a more than sufficient number of clients to validate their *raison d'être,* and are well able to survive without the patronage of any one individual. Hence, the client needs the agency more than the agency needs the client. In such a situation, agencies are not necessarily responsive to all who need service, particularly when responsiveness to a given client requires great effort. Rather, there is a tendency for agencies with large consumer populations to serve the "good client" and, perhaps unwittingly, to ignore the "hard-to-reach." The phenomenon, when noted in poverty programs, was termed "creaming the poor," [3] but it is hardly problem-specific. It extends to the powerless in general, whether poor, black, aged, or defined as mentally ill.

When the presumed complementarity of interest between client and agency breaks down (or never existed) and mediation fails, the client needs an advocate. As advocate of client interest, the social worker demands that the agency provide the client with the benefits to which he is entitled.

A fourth set of expectations for behavior can be organized under the role name "conferee." The social worker takes the role of conferee for the purpose of determining, with the client, the task to be accomplished and the course of action to be pursued. The social worker confers with the client, providing information on alternative actions and the possible consequences of each, and encourages the client to decide for himself which alternative, if any, is congenial to his needs and life style.

The four social work roles are elaborated in a later chapter.

To recapitulate, the principle of following the demands of the client task requires the worker consistently and systematically to look beyond the client to see if others are facing the same task, and to assume different roles at different times as he performs different types of activities (A-type, B-type, and D-type) with various configurations of people.

The following episode illustrates the principle of following the demands of the client task.

Mrs. Fuller asked the County Board of Assistance to help her sixteen-year-old son, Joe, who was experiencing difficulty at school. In reponse to her request, Mr. Rand, a social worker at the agency, goes to see Joe. He begins his activity in Quadrant A, and takes the role of conferee.

I met with Joe in his home one morning before he went to school. We sat across from each other at the kitchen table. I began by asking him if he had some idea about why I was there, and he said that he guessed so, that he had trouble with schoolwork. I told him that his mother had said he was, and asked him if the difficulty in school was worrying him. He shook his head slightly in an affirmative way and, not looking directly at me, asked me if I was going to get him into welding school. I said I didn't know and asked him if that's what he would like. He said he guessed so, but that he didn't know. He said he wasn't doing well in school. His speech was hesitant at this point. I said, "You seem as if you're not too sure of yourself." There was a long silence.

Joe broke the silence, saying that he knew some guys who were going to college and that's what he'd like to do but that it's impossible. I asked him if he meant his grades would get in the way, and he said that was partly it but that it was all because he can't read. He spoke slowly and hesitantly, but articulately. I remained silent, nodding my head in acknowledgment. There was another silence.

Again Joe broke the silence. "I really can't read," he said. "I can't even understand some of the instructions in shop 'cause I can't read." He said that in school they don't care if you don't learn as long as you stay out of trouble. "You stay out of trouble, you pass."

At this point, Mr. Rand looks beyond Joe to see if other students at Joe's school are in a similar predicament.

We talked about needing to know how to read, whether for welding or for college, and I asked Joe if he knew of other guys in a similar predicament. He said that he did, and I wondered whether he could talk to them about getting a group together for reading or whatever. He said he would try, and we ended with the understanding that we would get together again.

While Joe worked on getting some of the others who shared his plight, Mr. Rand moved from Quadrant A to Quadrant D, and shifted his role from conferee to that of broker.

I talked without success to the Educational Unit of the County Board of Assistance. This unit is set up to service the educational needs of all Public Assistance, Medical Assistance, or food stamp recipients in the county, a 50,000-plus population. The unit is supposed to deal with tutoring, liaison between school and parents, and whatever other needs may develop in the area of education. The unit consists of one caseworker with obviously not enough time even to consider the problem until maybe several months from now.

Later, I spoke with Joe's counselor at school. The counselor was not aware of the exact nature of Joe's difficulties but seemed interested in helping out. There was a class for improving reading, but it was, as a rule, not available to students as old as Joe and his friends. The counselor said he would look into making an exception, however. I said that I would talk further with Joe about it.

The term "exception" poses a dilemma, for it suggests that the service is a gift as opposed to an entitlement. In this instance it implies that, due to the good will of this particular counselor at this particular time, Joe and his friends will be taught to read. But others, who have a different counselor, or who have the same counselor but do not find reading a problem until next month or next year, may have no place to turn. In addition to the obvious need to redesign the school program so that students will learn to read before reaching the tenth grade, a high school reading program should be consistently and systematically available to all students who wish to use it. A structure is needed, and this leads directly to a discussion of the third practice principle.

The Principle of Maximizing Potential Supports in the Client's Environment. This principle suggests modification of existing structures and/or creation of new structures to meet human needs, and this embodies the essential thrust of the structural approach to social work practice. With respect to the preceding example, the worker may engage teachers and administrators in setting up a reading program in the high school. In a social agency where clients wait several weeks between their application for help and the beginning of service, and this lapse in time can be traced to cumbersome intake procedures, the worker may engage agency personnel in changing the procedures or creating a program to serve clients during those weeks of processing. As a third example, in order to counteract the debilitating effects of a schoolteacher's frequent disparagement of one or several black children, the worker may enlist the local butcher, grocer, and newspaperman to tell these children regularly that they are all right. In all these examples, the worker attempts to maximize potential environmental supports by either modifying an existing structure or creating a new structure. And in all these examples the structures involve others (nonclients) in behalf of clients, and can therefore be considered D-type structures. The telephone network described in Chapter 2, on the other hand, was comprised by the persons who directly benefited from it, and is therefore considered an A-type structure.

It should be noted that the creation of all A-type structures and such D-type structures as the corps of community men enlisted to counteract the teacher's disparagement of some children shifts the helping relationship from client-worker to neighbor-neighbor, and a neighbor-neighbor relationship has the potential advantage of endurance over time. This is not true of a client-worker relationship, which by its very nature must end.

The professional helping relationship is a temporary one, and an emphasis on changing existing structures and creating new structures to meet human needs recognizes this. The worker does not occupy the central position in the helping process. Instead, he changes structures and creates structures that can operate without him. In other words, the social worker works himself out of a job.

In sum, the principle of maximizing potential supports in the client's environment tells the worker not to occupy the central position in the helping process. Rather, the worker is directed to change and create structures to reduce the pressures on his clients—to meet social need through social change.

The following episode describes the process through which Operation Switchboard was created and illustrates the principle of maximizing potential environmental supports.

The first step in forming the self-help network to lessen somewhat the isolation and loneliness expressed by several clients of the Mental Health Center involved phone calls to potential candidates.

I called Mrs. M. and introduced myself as one of the social workers at the Mental Health Center. I said I wanted her to get involved in a kind of phone network where people call each other a few times a week to see how each other is doing. This would be a way of letting people feel that they have someone to talk to when things are on their mind. Mrs. M. said it sounded like a good idea. I said the first meeting would be November 9, at 1:00 P.M. She said she would come.

Not everyone responded as Mrs. M. did. Approximately half

of the people whom the social worker called refused to get involved, and several others said they "would see." Eight people agreed to come to the first meeting to find out more details.

At the first meeting, three people showed up. They all looked at me with some suspicion. I welcomed them and explained briefly the thought behind the program. I invited them to share with one another what they thought of the idea. All three seemed to agree that it sounded like a pretty good idea and began to share tentatively with one another their feelings of loneliness and isolation. . . . The meeting ended with exchanging phone numbers.

After the meeting, I called all of those who said they were coming or made some tentative commitment to come, to find out what happened and to encourage them to attend the following week.

At the second meeting, two of the original three members showed up, plus Mrs. M., who could not make it to the first meeting. I asked Mrs. H. and Mr. P. how things worked out for them this week. Mrs. H. said that Miss T. (who was not present at this meeting) did call her this week, but she never got to return her call because so many things came up. I asked Mrs. H. how she thought Miss T. may have felt about not being called back. She said she really did not know but that she would explain everything when she called her later today or tomorrow. I said that of course she cannot know for a fact how Miss T. may have felt, but if she were in Miss T.'s shoes, how may she have felt? She thought about this for a moment and said that she guessed she may have felt a bit hurt. I said yes, that could well be the case.

We talked a bit more about telephoning one another, and I asked Mrs. M. how she felt about the program, especially since she thought it was a good idea, but she did not care for the idea of people calling each other a set number of times per week. She thought this would mean that some weeks she would call someone just to fill a "quota," and not because she really wanted to talk to that person. I said I could see what she meant, but had she thought of it from the other person's point of view, the person expecting the call from her? Maybe the time she really does not feel like calling is the very time that person needs to get a call from her. She thought about this for a while and said, "You have

a point there." She added that she would like to have the telephone numbers of all the people so she could call not only the one
person she was responsible for, but the others as well. I said that
was a really good idea and that I would have them for her next
week.

I turned to Mr. P. and said that I was glad to see him this week,
especially since he did not know if he would come back, since his
wife may object to his getting calls from other women. (Last week
he said he may not be able to participate because of this.) He smiled
and said he told his wife what the program was about and she did
not seem to mind the whole thing. I said I was glad about that.
There was a short silence during which Mr. P. looked pensive. He
broke the silence by asking what was the "ultimate purpose" of this
whole program and why did I start it in the first place? I reviewed
the purpose as I saw it and asked Mr. P. what purpose he saw in it
for himself, since he is taking part in it. He thought for a while
and said it seemed to him that a program like this helps people
to come out of their shell. He went on to say, with much feeling,
that sometime when he talks to other people for any length of
time or over a period of a few days, they begin to look at him funny,
or ask his family what's wrong with him. "So I just withdraw,
and sit back and don't say nothing." I said to Mr. P. that it must be
very upsetting to be afraid to talk to other people. He said it
certainly was. I said it must also hurt to hear comments questioning
whether there was something about him that was not "right." He
said, "You're darn right it does." I said, "No wonder you withdraw." I asked Mr. P. how he felt talking right now. He said he
felt okay, that he likes the idea of this group coming together and
talking every week, but he is not ready yet to make phone calls.
"Let me go at my own pace." I said we will do exactly that, and
that I was sure all of us were more than happy to have him just
come to the group meetings for a while, knowing how he feels
about talking to other people. He seemed quite satisfied with this
arrangement.

Mrs. H. said she had called Miss T. to find out why she had not
come to the last meeting, but was unable to reach her. She said
she also called Mrs. M. and chatted with her for about an hour.
She said that Mrs. M. even put her two-year-old son on the phone
to talk. She said they both enjoyed the conversation.

As the telephone network continued to operate, members began to call each other on occasions other than those agreed upon.

The participants in the telephone network have been connecting well with one another on the outside. While they do not call each other every day, they do call one another a couple of times a week. Two of the women have started sewing together, and the third one may join them. They do call one another when one of them does not show up for the Monday meeting. Around the Christmas holidays they exchanged cards, and one member called another on New Year's Eve to wish him and his family Happy New Year. Attendance has been excellent on the whole, with members calling me when they cannot come for any reason. It is hard to say just what it is that is making them come to the meetings in rain, snow, and bitter cold.

In an effort to extend the network to include other lonely people who might benefit from such a self-help action system, the social worker introduced the idea at a staff meeting. These meetings had tended to be largely *pro forma,* and real issues of consequence to staff, clients, and the process of service delivery were rarely discussed. Staff members seemed distrustful of each other, and instead of collaboration, there was a series of inter-necine conflicts.

I outlined the whole program at a staff meeting and asked other staff members to keep the network and its rationale in mind and see if they come across any people who could benefit from this pro-gram. The announcement and request were met with the usual noncommittal silence and lack of interest, with an occasional, vague Mona Lisa smile on a few people's faces. The Element Head said the program sounded interesting and worthwhile, and that he was sure staff members would keep it in mind for possible referrals. I was not so sure at all, and I am certain that neither was he.

The worker's second attempt to involve other staff members

in locating isolated persons and connecting them via the telephone network took the form of individual contacts.

I began approaching individual staff members, reminding them of my concern and asking them whether they had come across any persons who could benefit from the program. The answer was invariably, "No," but they each gave me a verbal pat on the back as if to say, "That's nice, dear." Only one person showed any real interest, and has since referred one person to Operation Switchboard.

Since both efforts to involve other staff were unsuccessful, the worker stepped back to reassess the situation in order to determine yet a third strategy. She recognized that, except for herself, the staff was primarily oriented toward and engaged in providing therapy, and that she was proposing that therapists refer "their patients" to a nontherapy service. Perhaps the unspoken message was, "I have found a better way," which could be felt as a threat to the *status quo*. An additional obstacle was the apparent unwillingness of staff persons to help each other. In a setting where everyone is equal, "sameness" can become confused with "equality," resulting in a lack of role differentiation. So, too, equality can produce a kind of "status anxiety" [4] which may manifest itself in fear that helping a colleague may put him a little ahead of you. In other words, the social worker seemed to be asking other staff people to help her in a project that seemed to threaten the therapy model.

The social worker did have a continuing network that was serving a useful function for its members and could be expanded to include other clients. As staff time was limited, and staff was not able to serve all persons in need, the telephone network could actually help the staff by lightening the burden of attempting to see more clients than time allowed. Thus, the worker could *give* something to other staff members—a resource to help remedy some of the isolation their clients were ex-

periencing, and a service for people on the waiting list with
whom they were concerned yet did not have sufficient time to
engage in therapy. It was from this perspective that the social
worker made her third attempt to obtain the cooperation of
her colleagues in increasing service delivery to their clients.

In the staff meeting, I reviewed the history of Operation Switchboard, and gave a very positive report. I said I knew how hard
it was to serve the number of people each of them was trying to
serve in his limited time, and that I knew how much they cared
about providing service to as many people as possible. I said it
was because of this that I wanted to tell them about this resource
and make it available if they thought it could be helpful to any of
their clients. There was much more interest this time. One staff
person wanted to know the criteria for joining—neurosis, psychosis,
schizophrenia, or something else. There was much amazement
when I said the only criterion was possession of a telephone, and
that for people who couldn't afford a phone, the department of
public assistance could arrange for one to be installed since this was
a mental health service. While there was surprise at the thought
that clients could benefit from something other than therapy, staff
seemed willing to try. Several people asked if they could refer
clients they were seeing in therapy as well as those they were unable
to see, and I said they could refer anyone they thought would
benefit, that I respected their professional judgments.

As time went on, the members of Operation Switchboard
extended their contact with each other from phone calls and
weekly meetings to visits at each other's homes. The sense of
isolation decreased markedly, and members attempted to come
to grips with some of the social factors that fostered their
isolation.

Mrs. D. went on to say that she would like to invite Mrs. H. to her
house but she is afraid that she will be harmed coming into the
project where she (Mrs. D.) lives, being that Mrs. H. is white and
whites often get knocked down, or robbed. I said it must be difficult

for her to want to reach out to a friend in such a nice way and to have such fears at the same time. Mrs. D. looked sad and said it was really a shame to have things like that get in the way of friendship. I suggested that perhaps there was a way she could help insure Mrs. H.'s safety so that she could visit her. She thought for a few minutes and said she could tell Mrs. H. exactly at which entrance to be and she could meet her downstairs. Mrs. H. thought that perhaps she could meet her even at the corner or the bus stop. Mrs. D. said that was a good idea and decided to invite Mrs. H. as soon as she speaks to her on the phone.

And within the network itself, there were differences that had to be confronted. Obstacles to self-help had to be challenged by the worker even when the group would have preferred to deny their existence.

Shortly after the meeting began I informed the members of the group that the following week we would be joined by a new member, Mrs. B. Everybody seemed quite happy about this, and there was general agreement to the effect that it would be nice to have more members in the group. I told the group that I quite agreed and then turned to Mr. P. and asked how he felt about having another woman in the group, since right now he is the only man, with three women members and a woman worker. He laughed and said he felt fine about that and it will be all right to have another lady in the group. I turned to the women and asked if they had any thoughts or feelings about this. They agreed that they have felt very comfortable with Mr. P., that he was "open-minded," a nice person, and easy to talk to, that the fact that he was a man "made no difference." Mrs. D. said that "we all have common problems; that's why we are here and can help each other; it makes no difference whether you are a man or a woman." The other two women agreed with this. I said that there was much to what they were saying and that it must be good for each of them to hear that they can be accepted and cared for simply because they are people with human problems. But could they now try to put themselves in Mr. P.'s place and try to imagine how it would feel to be the only man in a group of five women? The women laughed, and Mrs. H. said she would love it since it would bring a lot of attention to her.

The other two agreed, and Mr. P. said laughingly that there was something to that, although he would prefer to be thought of as "just another member of the group." The women assured him that he was and that they treat him "exactly the same."

A bit later on I inquired as to how the telephone network is working. The three women told me who had called the other during the week. They seemed quite satisfied with the arrangement. I asked at this point if anybody had called Mr. P. There was a deafening silence and obvious discomfort. After a pretty long silence, Mr. P. admitted that he was more than equally responsible for this. "I really have not made an effort to call any of the ladies, except once when I called Mrs. H." Mrs. D. said that the women were just as responsible, since they have not called him. Mrs. D. said, "I guess we have not treated you as equally as we thought." Mr. P. said he doesn't blame the women for not reaching out to him, being that he has not really reached out to them. "Before I started coming here I was so withdrawn I did not want to talk to anybody. I feel different now and I think you have been very patient with me and let me go at my own speed. But I agree with the social worker that I can go a little faster now."

Mr. P. did "go a little faster," as he said he would. With the support of the members of Operation Switchboard who encouraged him, and who listened to his excited reports, Mr. P. volunteered his services on the men's ward of the hospital, and was accepted as an official volunteer—complete with badge, which he wore to every meeting. It may be the first palatable label that has been tacked on him in years.

The Principle of Least Contest. This directs the worker to exert the least pressure necessary to accomplish the client task. In the first place, force tends to generate counterforce. The amount of pressure that the worker brings to bear on a target system is directly related to the amount of counterpressure that the target system is likely to exert. And since low-pressure interventions tend to evoke minimum resistance on the part of the target system, low-pressure interventions are more likely to result in successful task accomplishment. Moreover, when low-pressure interventions are not successful, greater pressure can then be exerted.

The initial use of forceful intervention behaviors precludes the use of less forceful behaviors. It can be likened to "putting all the eggs in one basket," for in the event that the forceful intervention does not result in task accomplishment, alternative interventions are severely limited. To maximize the probability of task accomplishment, the worker should not act so as to preclude alternative actions. This suggests that the worker should serially order his possible interventions along a power dimension, from the least forceful to the most forceful.

With respect to types of activity, when task accomplishment demands a change in a particular procedure in a given agency, such as a lengthy intake procedure, the worker should try D-type activity prior to B-type activity. In other words, he should try to work with agency staff before organizing a client protest. The worker's own efforts with agency staff are likely to be less threatening than a client protest, and therefore less likely to generate the counterpressure that the more threatening client protest is likely to evoke. Further, in the event that D-type activity does not succeed, the worker can then move to B-type activity. The reverse is not possible, however, for the worker who has organized a client protest is no longer credible as a person who wants to help the agency.

Role-taking behavior is governed by a similar rationale. The worker should take the role of broker prior to the role of mediator, and the role of mediator prior to the role of advocate, for brokerage is less threatening than mediation, and mediation is less threatening than advocacy. Moreover, the worker who has attempted to mediate the client-agency engagement can, in the event that complementarity of interest cannot be implemented, shift from the role of mediator to the role of advocate. Again, the reverse is not possible, for the worker who has taken the side of one of two parties to a conflict has lost his credibility as a "neutral," or as a person equally concerned with both parties.

The same rationale holds for selecting a point of intervention into a bureaucratic system. An issue is of less moment when it is raised, and remains, at lower levels in the heirarchy, and increases in moment as it moves upward in the hierarchy. Therefore, the worker should escalate issues slowly, initiating action at the lowest possible hierarchical level, and proceeding upward until a concession is obtained. This process gives personnel at lower hierarchical levels an opportunity to contain the issue at the lower level by granting the concession, an opportunity which personnel in the highly political public welfare agencies are likely to seize. And if personnel at lower levels cannot or do not grant the concession, the worker can then escalate the issue to the next hierarchical level.

The principle of least contest, then, directs the worker to rank his interventions along a power dimension, and to use less powerful interventions prior to using more powerful interventions. Specifically, the worker should engage in D-type activity before B-type activity, take the role of broker before taking the role of mediator and the role of mediator before the role of advocate, and escalate issues slowly by intervening at the lowest possible hierarchical level in a bureaucratic organization and proceeding upward until a concession is obtained.

A graphic overview of all four principles and their operational definitions is outlined below:

THE STRUCTURAL MODEL: PRINCIPLES AND OPERATIONAL DEFINITIONS

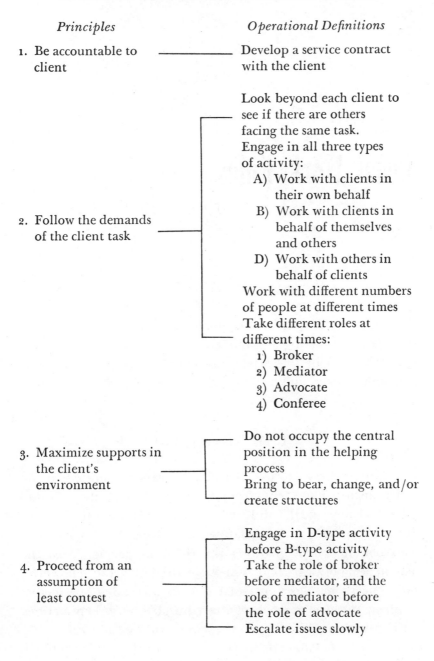

Principles	*Operational Definitions*
1. Be accountable to client	Develop a service contract with the client
2. Follow the demands of the client task	Look beyond each client to see if there are others facing the same task. Engage in all three types of activity: A) Work with clients in their own behalf B) Work with clients in behalf of themselves and others D) Work with others in behalf of clients Work with different numbers of people at different times Take different roles at different times: 1) Broker 2) Mediator 3) Advocate 4) Conferee
3. Maximize supports in the client's environment	Do not occupy the central position in the helping process Bring to bear, change, and/or create structures
4. Proceed from an assumption of least contest	Engage in D-type activity before B-type activity Take the role of broker before mediator, and the role of mediator before the role of advocate Escalate issues slowly

Chapter 5

Social Work Rules

A role is a set of expectations for behavior. To the extent that these expectations are clearly specified, behavior in accord with them is reliable, that is, consistent and stable. Prerequisite to systematic role-taking and role enactment in social work, then, is a definition of the expectations for the roles of advocate, mediator, broker, and conferee.

THE ADVOCATE

From the earliest efforts of social reformers committed to the social justice movement, from Dorothea Dix, Lillian Wald,[1] Jane Addams,[2] and Jacob Riis,[3] to the Mobilization for Youth [4] project in New York, social workers have been concerned with obtaining and guarding the rights of people. With the heightened political consciousness of the last decade, however, this concern has been articulated with increasing specificity,[5] resulting in the emergence of a recognizable set of expectations for behavior organized under the special rubric "advocacy."

According to Richan,[6] the basis for advocacy in social work is protection of client rights. That is to say, "the advocate steps in to help the individual victim or the class of victims obtain their entitlement."[7] In practice, that is largely an effort to make service systems (hospitals, housing authorities, schools, social agencies) more responsive to clients and their needs, but it could also include the unresponsive slumlord, the harried schoolteacher, the overprotective mother, or the corner grocer.

The role of advocate is predicated on the assumption of a conflict situation. Given that role-taking is reciprocal,[8] that people choose roles to complement the roles others have already taken, action on this assumption invites the target of action to take the role of adversary. If the target of advocacy accepts the role of adversary and plays it well, however, the goal will not be realized. This is the advocacy paradox. The social worker takes the role of advocate because he presumes the other to be an adversary, and in taking the role he initiates a process which could end in a self-fulfilling prophecy.[9] The encounter can quickly become a contest in which neither side can bear to lose. And it is the client who gets lost as each of the warring parties seeks total defeat of the other.

If the social worker is to maximize the client's opportunity to obtain his entitlement, he should take the role of advocate if, and only if, his activities in other social work roles (broker, mediator) have failed to produce the desired outcome. And when he does take the role of advocate, he must compensate for the reciprocal role message to reverse the self-fulfilling prophecy. Richan and Rosenberg allude to the need for compensation and provide some heuristics:

An important principle in advocacy is making it easy for the target system to say "yes." For instance, the put-down—humiliation of a decision-maker—may be personally gratifying to the advocate, but it is the surest way to build a wall of resistance. The advocate needs to be prepared to help the target system save face. Related to this is the need of the target system to justify its actions. The advocate can help in supplying the rationale for a positive response.[10]

In a bureaucratic organization, the power of the advocate is the potential power to escalate the problem, to raise it to higher levels in the hierarchy. Thus his point of entry into the target system is critical. To maximize this potential power, the advocate should enter the system at the lowest possible hierarchical level and proceed upward until a concession is obtained. The problem should be escalated slowly, with personnel at each succeeding level recognized and afforded ample opportunity to contain the problem at that level by making a positive response. This is consistent with the principle of least contest discussed in Chapter 4. In addition to maximizing the social worker's bargaining power, this procedure minimizes alienation of, and consequent subversion and/or retaliation against the client by, line workers who have to implement whatever concessions are obtained at higher levels.

When a concession is made and the benefits to which the client is entitled are obtained, it is imperative that the social work advocate shift his stance. He should engage the other as a partner in outrage over the violation of client rights rather than as a defeated adversary. While this is directed toward helping the other to save face, it is neither gimmickry nor manipulation. To the contrary, it is a human response to the human feelings which concession engenders. Goffman [11] has elaborated an array of strategies that are employed to help losers keep their self-image intact and adjust to situations following defeat or concession. Implicit in his discussion are such activities as listening, staying with the other, helping him get out his anger, helping him preserve the illusion that he wanted the change, and so forth.

Such deliberate shifts in the advocate's behavior not only help the one who has conceded to maintain his status, but they pave the way for important cooperative action to modify or create a structure through which all present and future clients can obtain their entitlement without needing an advocate. This is consistent with the principle of maximizing supports in the client's environment. From a structural perspective, the aim of advocacy is always universalistic as opposed to an exceptionalistic aim of obtaining this concession for this client at this time.

THE OTHER SIDE OF ADVOCACY

In general, the client of the social work advocate is relatively powerless. That is to say, his resources (money, political influence) are not equal to those of the withholding party. In fact, the client is frequently dependent upon the resources doled out by the more powerful party. Thus, while the consequences of not receiving a withheld benefit may be deleterious to the social welfare of the client, the consequences of opposing that powerful system upon which he is dependent may be even harder for him to bear. The tenant who engages in a rent strike against a slumlord who refuses to have faulty plumbing or wiring repaired, for example, may get the plumbing or wiring repaired, but may then have to live with such retaliatory measures as no heat, or eviction should a single rent payment be late. Worse yet, the strike may not be successful, and the tenants may have to bear the landlord's retaliatory action in addition to the faulty plumbing or wiring.

Since the social worker can never promise a successful outcome without repercussions, the client is often faced with what amounts to a Hobson's choice. And this is the basis for ambivalence on the part of the client in response to the social worker's offer of advocacy. There is a fearful "no" beneath his most enthsiastic "yes," and a "yes" beneath his most adamant "no." And because it is the client who must bear the consequences, it is the client who must decide whether or not to op-

pose the powerful other. It is therefore incumbent upon the
social worker to raise the other side of advocacy. That is, the
social worker should help his clients entertain the possibility
of defeat and recognize their ambivalence. He should provide
them with information regarding alternative actions from which
they might choose and the possible consequences for themselves
of each. The young adult who wants to move away from his
domineering parents, for example, has to entertain the possibility of needing money and having his parents refuse to provide
it, or needing to move back in and having to bear the "I-told-
you-sos." The social worker is ethically bound to engage the
client in a full discussion, even if—especially if—through the
process of that discussion the client decides "no." Perhaps this
is the hardest part for the enthusiastic and idealistic social
worker, but it speaks to the heart of client self-determination,
to a genuine respect for the right of people to decide their own
destiny.

TWO TYPES OF ADVOCACY

Should the client decide "yes," social work advocacy can take
either or both of two different forms. Using the Quadrant
model, we call these two forms D-type advocacy and B-type
advocacy. In the case of D-type advocacy, the social worker
argues for the client's entitlement. That is to say, he directly
engages the party or parties presumably violating the rights
of his client and intercedes in his behalf. In the case of B-type
advocacy, on the other hand, the social worker organizes those
clients whose rights in a given area have been violated and
mobilizes them to argue for their own entitlement. Whenever
a situation calls for advocacy, the worker needs to choose either
D-type, B-type, or some combination of the two.

Since the aim of advocacy is to obtain the benefits to which
the clients are entitled, we propose potential for accomplishing
this aim as the primary criterion for determining the particular

form of advocacy the worker should take in any given instance. Like all social workers, we value the positive experience which people can have as they work together and take action in their own behalf, even if they do not succeed in accomplishing their manifest task. But when the rights of people are at stake, we do not value the psychological experience above task accomplishment. In other words, when situational factors and political reality make D-type advocacy (see the principle of least contest) seem more strategic, we recommend that the worker use it, even though it may not promote the positive feelings associated with self-help. Moreover, we believe that the positive feelings associated with accordance of one's rights are more real and more lasting, irrespective of the extent to which one has obtained it through his own efforts.

THE MEDIATOR

Another set of expectations for behavior which has gained increasing recognition over the last decade is the role of mediator. Generally associated with its primary formulator, William Schwartz,[12] mediation is based on the concept of mutual aid from the social philosophy of Kropotkin.[13]

Whereas advocacy presumes a basic conflict between individual and social interest, mediation presumes a common bond. The common bond may be a complementary one, as the bond between client need and agency service, or it may be an identical one, as the bond between construction workers who need each other in order to obtain wage increases. Consistent with this, conflict is viewed as a sign that one or both parties to the encounter have lost sight of the need each has for the other, and signals an occasion for the performance of mediating behaviors.

It is the aim of the mediator to help the parties in conflict to rediscover their need for each other, thereby freeing them to contribute to each other's welfare. The mediator positions himself between the conflicting parties to help each reach out to the other for their mutual self-fulfillment.[14] In other words, the basis for mediation in social work is implementation of the identity or complementarity of individual and social interest where it breaks down or grows obscure.

The role of mediator can be defined in terms of five expectations for behavior: (1) identifying the common ground on which the two parties with their conflicting perceptions of self-interest can meet; (2) identifying the obstacles which are obscuring that common ground, such as authority problems, and challenging both parties to find a way around or through the obstacles; (3) defining the limits of the situation; (4) providing information; and (5) projecting an image of oneself as a person who stands for the welfare of both parties.[15]

IDENTIFYING COMMON GROUND

Common ground is a point of reference belonging to more than one person. It is an area of overlap between the self-interest of one person and the self-interest of another person. Where it can be recognized, it constitutes the basis of their need for each other and the motive for cooperative interaction.

In a corporate society where every person is part of a complex network of demand and relationship, the bond between individual and social interest grows diffuse and can easily be obscured in any particular instance of the individual-social encounter. When the social worker takes the role of mediator in order to implement the mutuality of interest between parties, therefore, he must begin by recognizing the point at which their apparently different self-interests converge. Having noted that point of convergence, the mediator talks with each of the parties individually, pointing out the stake each has in instituting a cooperative relationship with the other, and asking each to engage the other in order to effect such cooperation. He offers to help each party talk to the other, and should this be agreeable, establishes service contracts with both.

The second step involves a joint meeting in which the mediator points out the common ground on which the two parties can meet and establishes a service contract with them as a unit. He clarifies his stake in their engagement, indicating that he will help them do what they came together to do, that his interest is in their engagement rather than in any particular outcome. In other words, he sides with neither one party nor the other, but stands between them, equally concerned about both, and placing his faith in their engagement.

IDENTIFYING OBSTACLES

As two parties work to effect cooperative interaction, many obstacles can arise to block valid communication. Variables such as culturally based ethics, norms, and personal needs, for example, can intervene and obscure the common ground. Norms against comparing salaries can prevent employees from discovering and substantiating the existence of inequities, thereby hindering united action to rectify them. Likewise, norms that prohibit the open communication of emotion prevent essential information from being exchanged and can render a potentially meaningful relationship sterile. This is frequently a problem in marriage counseling, and much of the counselor's effort is directed toward increasing the flow of affect between husband and wife.

The prevalence of a win-as-much-as-you-can ethic in our society poses a constant threat to the integrity of cooperative efforts to obtain mutual self-fulfillment. It is not unlikely that either or both parties to the encounter will lose sight of the potential for mutual gain to the extent that each will consider losing some of what he already has won, so long as the other party loses more. Problems of authority also become obstacles to valid communication and mutual aid when they operate just beneath the surface. Manifest efforts to cooperate both hide and serve as the medium through which a counterproductive game of who's-on-top [16] is played.

When obstacles such as these subvert authentic efforts to cooperate, the mediator should indicate the obstacle and challenge both parties to deal with it openly and honestly. He should again point to the common ground and ask each if his need for the other is sufficiently strong to motivate him to find a way around or through the obstacle. In other words, the mediator forces underlying issues to the surface where they can be tackled with purpose and with affect.

DEFINING LIMITS

Every instance of the individual social encounter occurs within and is influenced by an institutional context. Contextual forces external to the particular encounter, such as time, money, and the demands of other relationship systems, impinge upon both parties and limit the nature and extent of their potential agreement and the conditions under which it can and cannot operate. If a student who wants to learn and a teacher who wants to teach recognize their need for each other, they can come to grips with and work through such an obstacle to their mutual self-fulfillment as problems of authority. But they cannot extend the teaching/learning time to include Saturdays, for example, without producing consequences for their respective family systems. Both parties must be aware of the boundaries beyond which their agreement produces consequences for other systems in their social networks in order for them to make choices and exercise some measure of control over their individual and mutual destinies. In order to guard the right of self-determination of both parties, the mediator should ask them to recognize the boundaries explicitly and to make their decisions in light of all foreseeable contingencies.

PROVIDING INFORMATION

Because people formulate issues based on the information (facts, opinions, ideas, feelings) they possess and choose actions from available alternatives, information is critical to decision-making. That is to say, the extent to which a person can make critical decisions about his own life depends upon the amount and kind of information which he possesses about the situation in which he is involved and the conditions under which that situation can be changed. In other words, information is a resource and, like any other resource, when it is differentially distributed, it produces power differentials.

When one of two parties to an encounter possesses relevant information which the other does not, the social worker in the role of mediator should help establish parity either by asking the one party to share his information, or by providing it for the other himself. What if the worker has access to relevant information which neither party to the encounter possesses? In this event, the mediator should provide both parties with the information so they will be neither dependent upon him every step of the way nor forced to make decisions without considering all possible data.

When the mediator provides information, particularly ideas, feelings, and opinions, it is important that he present it as his own rather than as an established "truth," and he should only provide information which has direct bearing on the issue at hand at the time it is at hand. Opinions presented as facts serve to distort and manipulate, and information that is not relevant, if it is heard at all, can divert the attention of the two parties from the particular piece of work in which they are engaged. If information is presented honestly and in a suitable manner, it can increase the power of people to exercise some measure of control over their relatedness to others and the outcome of this relatedness to their individual lives.

PROJECTING AN IMAGE

As indicated earlier, the mediator stands for the welfare of both parties to an encounter. He positions himself between them and acts to implement their presumed identity or complementarity of interest.

In siding with neither one party nor the other, but with the engagement itself, he announces his faith that the outcome of open and honest communication between people who need each other will be to their mutual benefit. And when he asks both parties to deal with the obstacles that block communication, he projects an image of himself as one who believes that such obstacles can be overcome, and that the need of people for each other is a sufficient motive for doing the hard but necessary work to overcome them. This is the image which the social worker as mediator must project, and this image is inextricably bound to the assumption of identity or complementarity of interest between parties. In other words, the social worker can take the role of mediator if, and only if, he presumes common ground. If he presumes a basic conflict of interest, on the other hand, he takes the role of advocate.

Since neither the assumption underlying advocacy nor the assumption underlying mediation accurately represents all instances of individual-social conflict, neither role is sufficient for all instances of social work intervention. Both roles are available to the social worker and, given the limits of his understanding in every situation, he must choose the role which seems fitting. Some guidelines are provided by the principle of least contest described in Chapter 4. Specifically, the worker who takes the role of mediator in a given situation, finds it insufficient, and cannot, after careful analysis, attribute that insufficiency to his own performance of the role, can shift to the role of advocate. The reverse is rarely possible, for the worker who sides with one of two conflicting parties has lost his credibility as a "neutral" equally concerned about the interests of both. As a rule of thumb, mediation should precede advocacy, and, as the following paragraphs explain, a third role, that of broker, should precede mediation.

THE BROKER

The basis for brokerage in social work is linking clients to community resources. This role presupposes a complementarity of interest between the client in need and the agency offering a service. Under ideal circumstances, the social worker taking the role of broker uncovers and clears the access routes between clients and the resource distributors, whose purpose is to meet various needs. In this role the social worker operates at the level of least contest; for assumedly, the service providers need populations to receive the services just as the populations need some place to turn for particular goods or services that the broader community has determined to disperse.

This is perhaps the oldest and best known social work role, dating back to the friendly visitors and settlement house workers of the turn of the century. The early caseworkers were experts in finding, interpreting, and creating resources for the needy. In fact, these activities comprised so much of the work that it hardly seemed necessary to attach a special theoretical importance to them. In large part, this was what any "good" caseworker did. Imbued with the spirit of social reform, the settlement house workers brought immigrants to English classes, alerted young adults of the ghetto to upcoming civil service tests, described the advantages of day nurseries and credit unions to the poor, and provided vacations in the country with lots of food, rest, and clean air for the mothers and children of the tenements. These early social workers also found "angels" to sponsor an aspiring young talent, told the ladies auxiliaries where to distribute the holiday dinners, and worked with politicians to get garbage removed, streets lighted, and clinics established.[17]

With urban life becoming increasingly complex, brokerage—concerned with exchange and transactions—performed either as a total occupation or as a part of an occupational interest can be found in many areas of society. The purpose of these intermediaries, go-betweens, or agents is to connect seekers with offerers in the worlds of commerce, business, and industry much as in social welfare. The cadre of experts who provide knowledge and resources in affairs of doing and being includes, for example, the public accountant who understands the tax requirements, the investment counselor, the real estate agent, the travel agent, the bridal consultants.

Within social work's relatively brief history, brokerage functions probably predominated up to the 1920s when casework shifted primary attention from the social realities to the internal dynamics of client problems.[18] Today, this role possesses least status in the eyes of many in the profession, probably since the mainstream interest of the profession from the 1940s to the mid-1960s was in professionalizing itself. Greater energy and theoretical interest surrounded "intensive" casework or "specialized" group work than the more mundane activities of referral or resource creation. Often, brokerage is the first role to be given away to others or to be sloughed off in the social worker's busy workaday schedule. Brokerage is barely discussed in the professional literature, minimally supported in funding, and hardly legitimated or sanctioned by the community through institutionalized, visible service components within the network of services.

However, the need for brokerage is today more acute than in the past, and new forms of brokerage have emerged to meet the demands of the urban scene. Community action groups, provided with momentum by the poverty programs of the 1960s, have seized upon brokerage services that provide visibility to the organization and inspire responsiveness in individuals who are either demoralized by the effort to gain access to the established bureaucracies or desperate with crises. Hot lines to reach the drug user, the suicidal, or the unmarried, pregnant teenager, for example, are springing up around the country. Many of these are staffed by volunteers devoted to a particular cause; others may employ professionals with specialized skills and a commitment to the validity of this role. In various communities trailers bring the broker to alienated teenagers, Vietnam veterans, and the people on skid row [19]— populations that might not take themselves to the offices of community agencies. The needs of people for goods and services have been and continue to be a major concern in social work.

If resources were available in abundance, well-known to all segments of the community, accessible without question, and offered without stigmatization, the role of the broker would be relatively easy. He would merely tell the resource seeker where the distributor is located. Since present social arrangements do not meet these conditions however, the complexities of the broker role are enormous.

The supposed complementarity of interest between client need and agency service often has broken down or has never existed in today's world of burgeoning social needs where the economic arrangements are based upon scarcity. Thus, brokerage must demand more than merely linking needs with resources. Within the reality of the social arrangements for service delivery, we propose three expectations for the behavior of the social worker taking the role of broker: (1) knowing the resources; (2) husbanding these resources; and (3) creating resources where there are none.

KNOWING THE RESOURCES

Knowing the resources of the community is more complex than may initially appear. Involved here is knowing what services are offered, how and to whom they are available, what demands are made upon the seeker, and other formal aspects of the service delivery pattern. In addition, the social worker needs to have an informal reading of the delivery system. That is, he needs to know what actually happens when a person tries to avail himself of that resource. Moreover, it is not enough to know the range of resources available within the network of social service agencies. If the broker is to be effective, he must be familiar with those offered under political auspices, by religious institutions, self-help organizations, schools, storefront programs, and through health delivery systems, and all other enterprises in both the public and private sectors of the community. In short, he should have the pulse of the community at his fingertips and he should constantly revise his inventory of resources and distributors in accord with information learned in his day-by-day contacts.

Knowledge about the diverse access routes to each resource is especially important, be this a generalized notion of the reception procedures or the name of a key individual. Such detailed information cannot be obtained merely from a directory of services. Entailed here is firsthand knowledge amassed from actual contact with the distributing agents and their resources. This means that one priority for the social worker is that of becoming personally acquainted with related service centers so that he knows exactly what he is talking about when he suggests various resources to his clients.

HUSBANDING THE RESOURCES

In addition to having up-to-date knowledge of community resources, the broker must attend to and cultivate them in the long-term interest of his clients. He should maintain contact with responsive systems and work to effect more responsive procedures in difficult systems at times when no client is in need and no particular crisis demands an immediate response. In the first place, such noncrisis-precipitated intersystem collaboration facilitates the efficient connection of client need to community resources in terms of the amount of time between a client's initial expression of need and service to meet his need. The broker confronted with a critical need for a particular resource can tap previously established channels rather than begin, at the point of crisis, the time-consuming search for, and effort to open up, a connection for the first time.

Moreover, noncrisis-oriented intersystem collaboration can be approached from a universalistic perspective. That is, the collaborative work can focus on developing structures that will endure beyond any single client and any single moment. Intersystem contact that is limited to points of crisis, on the other hand, must, of necessity, seek and settle for exceptionalism, for a special arrangement, so that only this particular client can get only this particular service at only this particular time. By implication, the client's need is an execptional one and could not have been predicted. And while this may be the case in some instances, human needs are largely universal and predictable, although programs to meet human needs are more often than not predicated on the fallacious assumption of exceptionalism.[20] If the social worker is to avoid perpetuating the myth of exceptionalism in his own practice, then, he will take the role of broker when he is not confronted with a client in crisis in order to create access roads through the network of community services—roads that will be open when any client needs to use them.

CREATING RESOURCES

The third expectation for the social worker as broker is that of developing resources where none exist. That a particular resource is needed may occur to the social worker in relation to a particular client's problem, or as a more generalized insight in the course of pursuing his professional assignment in a particular place within the service delivery network. Rather than dismissing the idea as impractical, impossible, too time-consuming, or an interesting notion for someone else to pursue, the social worker can and should lend his efforts to implementation of the idea. Since the broker stands at the interface between client need and community resources, he must do what needs to be done to induce the forces within the environment to produce resources. In other words, if there is no resource to serve the client, then part of the brokerage role must include the creation of a resource.

As suggested, the creation of a new resource begins with an idea about need and how it might be met. Once the idea has occurred to him, the broker must consider who else might be interested in it, and how those who are interested can be engaged as co-implementers, allies, or both. In some instances the clients themselves can be mobilized in their own behalf, as illustrated in the formation of the telephone network described in Chapter 4. In some instances the worker can organize others in the community to provide systematically a particular resource, such as the corps of community doctors cited in Chapter 2, who were enlisted to write prescriptions for community mental health center clients. In still other instances the worker can interpret the need to his own colleagues, organized groups in the community, legislators, and/or other funding sources in the interest of providing resources to meet client needs.

If the social worker's orientation includes helping others to provide resources for themselves and helping move potential allies to provide resources, new possibilities are immediately open. For example, one consultant was engaged by a school district to offer three sessions to school counselors from several high schools as part of upgrading their skills in using groups. In the final session it was obvious that the training was just taking hold and the counselors were operating as a group, enthusiastic about their learning experience. The impending end of the sessions was viewed with dismay by the counselors, who expressed grief and apprehension that they now had to "go it" alone. In the final session, the consultant helped the group plan to meet independently as a self-help seminar. The final part of the training session was devoted to helping the group organize itself, distributing responsibilities for conducting the next meetings, planning a sequence of content to move into, and developing some new morale in anticipation that they could keep learning by means of certain additional structures and ground rules suggested by the consultant.

In taking the role of broker, the social worker must know both the formal and the informal aspects of obtaining resources from various agencies; he must husband these resources, maintaining contact with responsive agencies and effecting more responsive procedures in difficult agencies; and he must work to create resources when there are needs but no services to meet them. But let us assume, now, that the social worker knows of a suitable resource to meet a client's need and has maintained a working relation with the agency. When the client is referred to the service, it is incumbent upon the one in the brokerage role to stay by him until the linkage with the service is accomplished. In some instances this new connection will spell the end of the brokerage and the work with the client. Sometimes there are other tasks that require the attention of both client and worker at the time the client also moves to another service. In such instances a new contract is made, and the worker continues to meet with the client and/or others in his life who are important to the ongoing tasks. In other situations, the client returns with his version of what happened or did not happen when he sought help from a specified resource. Perhaps the agency was unresponsive. The social worker's role might now shift to mediator in order to explore the blockage to an effective contact or to an advocacy role to bring pressure upon the resource to be more responsive.

Clearly, brokerage implies analysis of the situation after the referral is made, for the work is not over until some response from the other distributors of services is made. Perhaps alternative resources may be proposed if the first referral failed; or increased pressure may be applied to an unresponsive resource. In the brokerage role, the social worker can gather data that can be gleaned only from operating at the interface between persons in need and community response. Such data can be used to inform the policy-makers of the plight of all those who slip through the holes within the network of resources and thus lead to the creation of systems more prepared to accommodate those who need services. In fact, being skillful and thorough at this level might bring about a lessened need for activity by social workers in roles of increased pressure.

ROLE ASSUMPTIONS AND
ROLE-TAKING BEHAVIOR

In the foregoing definition of expectations organized under the roles of advocate, mediator, and broker, the assumptions which underlie each role were described. These assumptions are the organizing principles for role expectations and constitute the criteria for determining the appropriateness of a given role in a given situation. That is to say, a role is appropriate to the extent that the situation meets the assumptions underlying that role. The role of advocate, for example, is not suitable in a situation in which interests are complementary and that complementarity is operational. In such a situation the most feasible social work role is that of broker, for brokerage presupposes an operational complementarity of interest. Advocacy, on the other hand, presumes a basic conflict of interest. Table 1 shows the three roles that have been defined thus far and the assumptions that indicate each.

TABLE 1
ROLES AND ROLE ASSUMPTIONS

Assumptions	Roles
Operational complementarity of interest	Broker
Nonoperational identity or complementarity of interest	Mediator
Conflict of interest	Advocate

It should be noted that the order of the roles in Table 1 reflects the principle of least contest (see Chapter 4). That is to say, the assumption indicating the role of broker organizes expectations for behavior in situations of lesser contest than does the assumption indicating the role of mediator; while the assumption indicating the role of mediator organizes expectations for behavior in situations of lesser contest than does the assumption that indicates advocacy, but of greater contest than the assumption indicating brokerage.

THE CONFEREE

The label of "conferee" distinguishes a fourth set of expectations which social workers act to fulfill in certain situations. "Conferee" stems from the notion of the conference, that encounter where two or more persons consult together, compare opinions, deliberate, and devise actions to be taken after the conference. A basic assumption underlying this role is that all parties have an equal obligation actively to determine subsequent action. Key concepts inhering in such a role, then, are mutuality and partnership. When the social worker assumes the role of conferee, the reciprocal role which the client must assume is also that of conferee.

The social worker, with the special knowledge and skill acquired through his professional education and experience, and the client, with his special knowledge of his life situation and all that it takes to live his life, consult together to decide what ought to be done and what each can and will do to reduce the pressures which the client is experiencing. To insure the integrity of the conference, the social worker must take his role as conferee through behaviors which clarify for the client that he too is a conferee, that he is not in a one-down position even if he expects and has had more experience with a one-down position. In other words, it is the responsibility of the social worker as conferee to initiate and maintain through all that he says and does that the client too takes the role of conferee. It is the social worker who must set this role relationship in motion.

Earlier it was suggested that every instance of social work in social service delivery begins in Quadrant A, that is, in work with specific clients out of concern with their plight. At this point it should be noted that in every instance of social service delivery, the worker begins by taking the role of conferee. That is to say, he starts with the client, listening as the client describes his situation, the pressures he feels, and what, if any, part of it he may want help with. Clients do not ask the worker to "be my broker" or "be my advocate." They talk about what is going on in their lives, how they feel about their life situations, and what they think will make a difference for them.

Thus, when client meets social worker, their relationship is that of conferees who will engage in activities surrounding task specification for each, pursuing the work to be done together and separately, and will conclude their contact with each other when the mutual work is over. The conferee role with any given client may be brief and lead quickly to the social worker's assumption of broker or mediator or advocate roles as determined by initial exploration of the plight of the client. As the work proceeds, the movement back into the conferee roles may punctuate task accomplishment as various facets of the client's situation are engaged. As such the conferee role has a linkage relationship to the other roles and threads through the rest of the work, prominent mainly at the beginning and at the ending phases of the contact. In other instances, the conferee role may be the primary one, particularly when the major concern or pressure upon the client is the determination of what action(s) he wishes to take to resolve his difficulties.

The conferee role, like the other roles discussed, is operative in all quadrants of activity, but we shall emphasize here the conferee role in Quadrant A. In Quadrants D and B the behavioral expectations for the social worker as participant with others in conferences guided by the assumptions of mutual and equal responsibility for involvement are quite familiar, as for example in team meetings, collaborative meetings, case conferences, and the like.

In Quadrant A, then, the social worker as conferee must set the stage and clarify with the client how they will work together. Rather than social worker being one-up and client one-down, their positions are side by side. Often the transaction occurs by means of an interview, which, if taken in its original meaning, sheds light on the nature of the interaction: to interview is to see each other, to have mutual sight. A significant difference bound up in the conferee designation resides in the partnership implied in its execution, in contrast, for example, with the role labels of "counselor" or "therapist" which specify a different power balance: knowledgeable worker and less knowledgeable client.

Three major expectations comprise the activities of the so-

cial worker as conferee: (1) translating pressures into tasks;
(2) exploring alternative courses of action and their consequences; and (3) determining when the work is over and
concluding the contact with the client. These same expectations
are equally applicable to the client in his role of conferee.

TRANSLATING PRESSURES INTO TASKS

In some instances the social worker is but one more in a long
line of social workers who have touched the life of the client
and/or his acquaintances. In this event, it is likely that the
client has formed his own picture of what social workers do
or do not do. It is likely, too, that he has an elaborate set of
attitudes about social workers in general, and that he brings
these attitudes to the first encounter. In the role of conferee,
the social worker may need to help the client sort out and
claim the preconceptions and previous experiences that condition what he thinks and feels about the possibilities of their
work together prior to the more specific work of agreeing on
the tasks to be accomplished and establishing a service contract.

Thus the first expectation for the social worker as conferee
is to help translate the pressures on the client into tasks to
lessen them. Preliminary within this expectation are those
orienting and stage-setting activities geared to acknowledgment
of preconceptions and prior experiences which condition the
client's view of the situation. This is not to imply that the social
worker builds a relationship first and then works on determining the tasks to be accomplished next. Rather, as part of that
process, the possible barriers to such work are engaged in order
for the conference to proceed. The following example recorded
by a social worker in the probation office of the county court
is illustrative:

A client came into the office saying that he had been told by the secretary in the
front office to report to either K. or T. (Last names only were used.) As Mr. K.

was speaking with another client, I got up, walked over to him and introduced myself. The client looked a bit startled. I asked him if he would like to have a seat and I proceeded to get out his file. The client sat down rather rigidly without removing his coat. A look of disgust came over his face, and he began to stare straight ahead, avoiding all eye contact. He mumbled an "umph." "Mr. J.," I said. He responded with another grunt. Again I tried, "Mr. J., you look uncomfortable. Does it bother you that I am a woman?" Mr. J. did a double-take and immediately looked at me. He responded, "Yes. I'm used to reporting down here, but I'm not used to speaking with a lady other than a secretary."

Obviously, this kind of exchange is necessary in order for the social worker to earn the right to work with the client. The need for such stage-setting activities is apparent at the outset for any new engagement and is especially highlighted with nonvoluntary clients or in instances when the social worker meets clients or potential clients on their home territory.

As part of the first phase of the work, the establishment of the service contract, the social worker attends to the atmosphere of the exchange, to the climate that surrounds the initial engagement. The activities involved in establishing the service contract have been discussed in Chapter 4, and these become the central focus in translating client pressures into tasks for client and social worker to pursue.

EXPLORING ALTERNATIVE COURSES OF ACTION AND THEIR CONSEQUENCES

A second expectation for the behavior of the conferee is that of exploring with the client a range of alternative courses of action and their possible consequences. It is out of such deliberation between worker and client as conferees that the service contract is initially established, subsequently changed, and finally terminated.

Central to this phase of the work is the decision-making process which contains both rational and emotional elements. Throughout the conference process, the worker should encourage the client to make his own decision rather than a decision which others may want him to make. The worker should encourage the client to consider alternatives in light of the possible consequences of each, the client's own feelings about what he can and cannot bear, his own assessment of what is and is not congenial to his cultural and individual values and life style, and to choose the course of action that he considers best for himself, irrespective of what that decision might be. The social worker as conferee does not attempt to influence the client to choose the alternative which he (the worker) thinks is best, nor does he judge the client from his own frame of reference. He does not evaluate the client's ability to make decisions based on how similar the client's decision is to the worker's own preferred course of action or personal values. Rather, the worker recognizes that the decision belongs to the client and only to the client, because the consequences are the client's and only the client's to bear.

Included in this phase of the work is the determination of what part of the client's pressures need to be considered first, the running out of possible actions the client wants to take or wants the worker to take, the anticipation of possible outcomes of various separate and/or joint actions, the determination of how much action the client is willing to take in his own behalf, and so forth. And as the conferees think about and take steps to act in a series of possible moves, they are testing out action against the backdrop of the client's social reality and making decisions that will affect this social situation. As part of this process, the client gains confirmation from the worker, through their joint deliberations and actions, that he is not alone with his problems or feelings.

Because decision-making is never a purely rational process, it must be understood that feelings and attitudes will arise to distort, elaborate, and modify facts as work on the contract

proceeds. Thus the social worker as conferee must be prepared
to engage his own attitudes and feelings, and to help the client
do the same. More specifically, the worker must raise both the
positive and the negative feelings that the client may be experiencing, although not expressing. He may need to help
the client understand that it is all right to have feelings and
that facing these, whatever they are, will be necessary in deciding on some action, hard as this is sometimes. And if the
client expresses only one side of his feelings, the social worker
should raise the less known ones that might also be there, for
these become part of the information on which the client can
ultimately base his decision.

All decisions are heavily influenced by attitude, past experience, emotion, and even intuition and hunches. Recognizing and facing these influences that lie in the emotional
realm proceed along with recognizing the problems and possible actions. For example, there may be eagerness yet fear
involved in taking a new job or in trying a new attitude
with others, and both elements involved in a new shift would
need to be faced and explored as part of the client's choice.

CONCLUDING THE WORK

The third expectation ordering the behavior of the conferees
is the determination of when the work is over and their contact
concluded. Much as they begin their work together by mutual
consent through the conference process, so do they end their
work together by mutual consent through the conference process, and each goes his separate way. The ending is apparent
when the tasks are accomplished or when the parties agree
that the work should be concluded.

As with all other aspects of the conferee process, the mutuality is central to the ending phase, but the client plays the
primary role in signaling the end. As he is central in defining

the pressures upon him at the outset, so is he central in determining the need to conclude. And while, in some instances, the social worker may see much more that could be engaged and worked on, he takes his cue from the client's perception of the degree and scope of involvement he sees for himself, and adjusts his view to the client's vision.

Part 2
Social Work Skill

Chapter 6

Introduction to Skill

Practice principles provide elements for the social worker to consider in the performance of his professional assignment, and they limit the range of alternative actions available to him.[1] The development of social work skill involves learning to produce specific behaviors through which the knowledge and values incorporated in, and organized by, the principles that guide practice can be applied in the performance of tasks.

There is increasing recognition in the professional literature that much of what has been presented as worker behavior is more accurately a group of goals to which some unspecified worker behavior should be directed. But, as Briar and Miller indicate:

Injunctions to "give support to the client" or to "clarify the client's feelings" are of little use unless the theory specifies, in terms of behaviors to be performed by the practitioners, how support may be given or how feelings may be clarified. . . . "Support" and "clarification" describe effects, not the actions to be taken to produce them. Such prescriptions amount to telling the practitioner to "make the client feel better," or "improve the client's social functioning."[2]

It is not sufficient to specify outcomes toward which unspecified behaviors should be directed. The behaviors must be specified, and the conditions that occasion their use must be explained. In terms of Argyle's wonderfully basic description of social interaction as the production of a series of noises and gestures in response to a series of noises and gestures produced by another,[3] the particular noises and gestures that the social worker should produce in response to particular noises and gestures produced by others under specified conditions must be made explicit. The effort here is to specify behavior through which the social worker can apply the principles of structural social work in response to the demands of people needing help with various problems.

In the following chapters, twenty-seven specific behaviors and the conditions that occasion their use are elaborated and illustrated. That is to say, each of these behaviors should be produced if, and only if, certain conditions obtain. The conditions signaling use of each behavior are indicated along with descriptions and illustrations of the behaviors. For conceptual clarity, the twenty-seven behaviors are grouped into six areas of skill: (1) stage setting; (2) attending; (3) engaging feelings; (4) engaging information; (5) managing interaction; and (6) engaging barriers. "Stage setting" designates behaviors for initiating interaction. "Attending" refers to the taking in of sensory data. "Engaging feelings" and "engaging information" involve behaviors dealing with the affective and informational content of messages. "Managing interaction" includes behaviors to monitor the flow of messages, while "engaging barriers" includes behaviors aimed at reducing or removing obstacles to task accomplishment. The behaviors comprising each area of skill are listed below:

Stage Setting

1. Positioning
2. Engaging in the medium of the other
3. Proposing a medium presumably congenial to the other

Attending

(Only one attending behavior is specified here; hence the category name, "Attending," is used to indicate the behavior as well.)

Engaging Feelings

1. Reaching for feelings
2. Waiting out feelings
3. Getting with feelings
4. Reporting own feelings
5. Reaching for a feeling link

Engaging Information

1. Reaching for information
2. Partializing
3. Giving information
4. Running out alternatives
5. Pointing out possible consequences
6. Connecting discrete events
7. Recasting problems
8. Summarizing

Managing Interaction

1. Checking out inferences
2. Giving feedback
3. Redirecting messages
4. Amplifying subtle messages
5. Toning down strong messages
6. Talking in the idiom of the other

Engaging Barriers

1. Referring to contract
2. Pointing out obstacles
3. Challenging taboos
4. Confronting with contradictory reality

This is not to imply that the six areas of skill are exhaustive; nor that the twenty-seven behaviors in the six areas of skill are all-inclusive. To the contrary, this is only a beginning move toward greater precision in social work practice.[4] Other behaviors have yet to be isolated, identified, and thereby made available for systematic use under specified conditions. And as other behaviors are defined and classified, it is likely that additional areas of skill will emerge. Ultimately, the validity of the classification scheme can be tested via a factor-analytic technique.

When many other specific behaviors have been isolated and explained, it should be possible to determine both the frequency with which each behavior is used, and differences in frequency of use as a function of (1) quadrant of activity: A vs. B vs. D; (2) role: broker vs. mediator vs. advocate vs.

conferee; and (3) configuration: dyad vs. triad vs. small group vs. large group. Thus behaviors specific to certain quadrants, roles, and/or configurations can be distinguished from generic behaviors. It should also be possible to identify use units, clusters of behaviors that tend to be used in sequence, and to determine how sequencing differs as a function of quadrant of activity, role, and configuration. Through such investigation, the interrelationships among components of the practice model can be specified with greater precision; hence practice can be more systematic.

As defined here, "skill" refers to the production of specific behaviors (reaching for a feeling link, checking out inferences) under the precise conditions designated for their use. In this sense, a worker cannot have more or less skill in producing a particular behavior. He either produces the behavior when presenting conditions signal its use, or he does not.[5] The worker can, however, have more or less skill in a given skill area (managing interaction, engaging barriers), and the degree of skill that the worker demonstrates is measurable. That is to say, worker skill in a given area is a direct function of the number of specific behaviors in that area that the worker produces under appropriate conditions. A worker who produces six of the eight information-engagement behaviors when presenting conditions signal their use is 75 percent skillful in engaging information. He is 25 percent more skillful than another worker who only produces four of the eight information-engagement behaviors under appropriate conditions.

It should be noted that production of a specific behavior under the precise conditions designated for its use involves two variables: knowledge and action. The worker must know the relationships between antecedent conditions, acts, and probable outcomes, on the one hand, and he must be able to produce the acts on the other hand. It is one thing to know that, given conditions a, b, and c, the use of behavior x will probably result in outcome y. It is quite another thing actually to produce behavior x. That is to say, while knowledge is necessary, it is not sufficient. Both knowledge of the conditions under which x will probably result in y and the ability to produce x are required. It follows that worker behavior can be viewed as hypothesis testing. In other words, every time the worker selects and produces a particular behavior, he is testing an hypothesis that the particular behavior he chose will produce the effect he desired. It follows, too, that whenever the worker's hypothesis is not confirmed, he will need to consider whether failure to obtain the expected outcome was a function of chance, whether an untenable hypothesis, or his own inaccurate production of the behavior he had properly chosen.

ANALYTIC BEHAVIOR

Underlying all decisions regarding intervention is a process of analysis, a series of cognitive behaviors aimed at answering the question: What is happening here? This question is simultaneously directed at two levels: (1) the continuing patterns of action and interaction in the social context, and (2) the momentary action-reaction sequences that occur within the restrictions imposed by the larger social context. On one level, analysis is of the social system, of the roles, rules, and processes with which the people within given boundaries are engaged. On the other level, analysis is of the momentary situation and takes the form of explanation by analogy.[6] In this latter instance, the question becomes: What does the current situation remind me of? And the answer is sought from among the paradigms with which the worker is familiar: this interaction looks like the final play in a con game with one of the operators "cooling the mark out"; [7] or this interaction reminds me of a courtroom with two antagonists wanting me to judge who is right.[8]

Since analysis is a cognitive process, hence not directly observable, it is especially difficult to isolate the specific components comprising analytic skill. It is nevertheless possible to describe some of these, at least in a general sense, that should be involved in a deliberate effort to understand what is happening in a given situation at a given time. It seems reasonable to assume, for example, that analysis of a situation requires a search for key variables, for those variables so central to the situation that if the observed values were to change, there would be a significant change in the situation. It is likely, too, that the search for key variables would be followed by combining variables, ordering the key variables into a composition that explains the observed phenomenon. This involves placing a frame of reference (a theory) on observed data that imparts meaning to the situation. Given that every theory is predicated on the cultural and personal biases of the theorist (see Chapter 12), it seems important to prescribe recombining variables as a check on combining variables. Recombining variables involves reordering the key variables into alternative compositions, each of which provides an alternative explanation of the observed phenomenon, by placing alternative frames of reference on the data. With respect to the momentary situation, on the other hand, explanation takes the form of analogy, suggesting that workers also reach for analogues, for analogous compositions of those variables central to a current situation that have been stored in memory.

At least three other components of analysis are worthy of note. First, looking for patterns of interaction seems necessary to an understanding of the social context which influences momentary behavior. Second, it seems important to listen for content themes, for the recurrent motifs expressed in various overt and/or covert forms, for these themes frequently point to areas of concern for those who are expressing them. Likewise, the worker should also look and listen for metamessages which frequently underlie overt expressions to the contrary. Where these analytic components seem prerequisite to the observable behavior delineated in the following chapters, we examine them in greater detail.

In chapters seven through ten, the six areas of skill mentioned earlier are described, and the specific behavior compressing each is explained. Each explication of a specific behavior includes the definition of that behavior, the conditions that signal its use, and illustrations of its application in practice.

Chapter 7

Skill in Stage Setting and Attending

Stage setting is the beginning. Included here is social worker behavior aimed at launching the interaction process. At the outset of every human exchange the worker's objectives include: (1) making the physical environment (spatial arrangements, privateness, setting) conducive to the anticipated interaction; and (2) providing a social-emotional environment congenial to connection or rapport. A theatrical metaphor has been used by others concerned with social interaction to describe "actors" in real-life "dramas," [1] and stage setting fits the purpose here of directing worker attention and actions to the set, the arrangements between worker and other(s) as the curtain rises.

Impressions begin on both sides as soon as the two parties are within visual range, and are continuously interpreted by each of the actors as signals of inviting or repelling intent. Through particular actions the worker can make a difference in the quality of each of his exchanges, whether with clients or with others in the service delivery system. In interactions with clients, his focus is upon the means through which he can increase client comfort. With respect to exchanges on a staff or interorganizational level, his focus may be upon the means through which he can increase the comfort or discomfort of the other, or assume the initiative or control. In general, the worker enacts certain behaviors in order to set the stage in a particular way. These behaviors convey messages about how potentially responsive or unresponsive the worker may be, how pleasant or unpleasant the exchange may be, the size of the social barrier between worker and the other, and the role the worker may wish the other to assume.

Skill in stage setting refers to the use of three specific behaviors: (1) positioning, (2) engaging in the medium of the other; and (3) proposing a medium presumably congenial to the other. These three behaviors will be further described and shown in examples.

POSITIONING

To position is to place one's self physically at the distance and/or angle suitable for a particular type of interaction and to adjust one's self in accord with ensuing cues from the other as the interaction continues. Distance ranges for various levels of personal involvement have been found to follow culturally determined norms [2] that offend the other if violated. Studies of personal space, that private area surrounding the person which others may not enter,[3] indicate that intrusion affects feelings of comfort and status.[4] There is also evidence to suggest that what is felt as intrusion differs as a function of other variables. That is to say, if one person sits near another, it makes a difference whether there are other seats he could have chosen, whether he is directly facing the other or at a right angle to him, and whether there is any physical barrier between them.[5] Likewise, studies of groups reveal the importance of position at a table (as well as the shape of the table) with respect to leadership and dominance, the amount of communication that will be directed to an individual, and involvement with particular others.[6] Additional aspects involved in positioning pertain to the person of the worker: his facial expression, his body posture, the direction in which he looks, and his general orientation to the other.

In the following episode the worker deliberately arranges herself in a knee-to-knee informal position, one found to be preferred by interviewees.[7] She does not assume a more formal, face-to-face position, an arrangement found preferable for competitive situations; [8] and she avoids the desk, a potentially separating middle-class and business-like accouterment, out of her concern for client comfort and awareness that desks may be physical and cultural barriers to interaction.

Mrs. K. came into my office and sat down. *I moved my chair from behind the desk* to cut down the psychological distance between us and sat near her.

In the next example, the worker initiates contact wit ha student in a classroom by assuming a side-by-side position, one used for very informal, transitory communications [9] as when watching and/or discussing something outside the individual. Then he shifts to a right angle to the student so that he can look directly at him, but the student can choose whether or not to become directly engaged with the worker. Since eye gaze is a powerful means of initiating interaction [10] but also a means for threatening or challenging,[11] the worker's behavior left choices and a space of freedom for the student.

I entered the ninth-grade classroom and noticed a new student in the class so *I sat next to him, placing myself parallel then twisting in my seat so I was positioned at a right angle to him.* Thus, he could choose when to have eye contact.

The following instance illustrates the approach-avoidance maneuvering that goes on constantly between workers and clients, often more disguised by the client as he covers up his responses. Here, the client is seated on the floor in a mental hospital day room as the worker approaches. The worker, aware that he is looking down on him, and conscious of the extra domination implied in such a position, squats and attempts to meet him intimately, face to face, on the same plane. Failing in this move, he then retreats to a side-by-side, less confronting position at a "casual-personal" [12] distance so that he might pose less threat.

Mr. A. was sitting on the floor of the day room with his knees drawn up to his chest. *I bent down in a squatting position directly in front of him,* and said, "Hello." Mr. A. immediately cringed and lowered his head. Upon viewing this, *I moved to a position alongside Mr. A., leaving about four feet of space between us, and sat down.*

Obviously, Mr. A. was not ready for this invasion of his personal space, and the worker, grasping his message, controlled his own positioning behavior out of consideration for client comfort.

These illustrations have dealt with social worker behavior intended to consider the comfort of the client. In some instances, however, especially with colleagues or superiors, the worker may adopt positioning behavior expected to generate the opposite of warmth, concern, openness, and nonsuperiority. The following example illustrates such positioning at a staff level. Here, the worker deliberately times his entrance into a staff meeting so that he can sit in the most powerful spot at the table. He is interested in seizing control of the meeting and knows that leadership can best be exerted from the head seat where he can look at everyone at once.[13]

Anticipating a power struggle, *I arrived at the task force meeting early in order to occupy the seat at the head of the table.*

The final illustration deals with an interaction in which the supervisor is intimidated by the positioning behavior of the worker although he may not be conscious of the source of his vague discomfort. In this instance, it is the worker who exerts the upper hand while he asks the supervisor to be more considerate of staff opinion.

Although many potential clients do not receive service because they work during the day, my supervisor had not been responsive to staff suggestions about keeping the Center open in the evening. Hoping to influence him, *I pulled my chair up close to him and faced him directly.* As I spoke, *I leaned forward and inched my chair further into his space.* He leaned backward slightly, rolled his chair back a little (*I inched my chair forward more*), and said that maybe it's a better idea than he initially thought.

ENGAGING IN THE MEDIUM OF THE OTHER

To engage in the medium of the other is to parallel what the other is doing, an act which often leads to verbal exchange. This behavior is fitting if, and only if, its use presumably increases the comfort of the other. For many different reasons (cultural, psychological, age, class, and status variables), some clients may be more comfortable in expressing themselves if approached in other than verbal behaviors. Sometimes a client is unwilling or uninterested in talking with the worker, perhaps feeling that verbal exchanges put him at a disadvantage.

Children, in particular, are much more communicative through actions than through words and are often able to express themselves more effectively through action or through pieces of verbal exchange "on top of" the action.[14] Often individuals feel most at home when engaged in a medium whose interactional rules are well-known (perhaps guided by ritual, tradition, or prescribed ground rules). Such "first-order communications" may be preferred because they enable the other to recognize easily what he and others are doing, and understand from his own experience the next interactional steps and necessary role performances.[15] In performing known functions, such as making a bed, playing a game, emptying trash, walking, an individual can feel at home and accommodate to a social worker who takes part in the act. It is here, then, that certain worker-client interactions must begin. By engaging in the medium of the other, such as doodling next to a doodling individual, digging in the sand with someone who is already digging there, or sitting silently next to a person wrapped in silence, the worker sets the stage for a connection with the client that is necessary in order to work on the task at hand.

In the following illustration the social worker initiates interaction with a young child by joining the activity of interest to her at the moment. Through this parallel behavior the worker is communicating, "I am interested in you."

During the free play period Bernice, a third-grader, stood all alone looking sad, petting a rabbit in a cage. I too walked over to the rabbit's cage, sat down, and *began to pet the rabbit.* I waited for Bernice, if she wanted to, to begin to talk with me.

In the second example, the worker notices that her client is reading a magazine. While Mrs. B. is engaged in her solitary activity, the worker operates with the knowledge that she is the intruder into Mrs. B.'s life space. It is she who is seeking something with Mrs. B.; Mrs. B. seems accepting of her solitary activity. The worker considers where she should position herself vis à vis Mrs. B., and times her entrance into Mrs. B.'s life carefully by reading her own magazine and sitting for a while near by before venturing a verbal exchange.

When I walked into the day room Mrs. B. was looking at a magazine. I sat down next to her, *picked up a magazine and began to look through it also.* Occasionally I would look away from the magazine and I noticed peripherally that when I looked away, she would move the magazine slightly so that she could see me. Finally, she put the magazine down and I did too. I waited a long time before speaking and then I said softly, "Sometimes it's hard to talk." She nodded and looked at the floor.

The stream of life in institutions goes on whether or not the social worker is present. Often, it is the social worker who is perceived as an outsider, both by residents *and* custodial staff, and who must make his entrance into the twenty-four-hour-a-day interactional network with care.

In the third example, the social worker becomes engaged with a client by sharing his silence.

When Mr. J. said that the Parole Board said no, he just sat there staring straight ahead of him. I sat down alongside him, leaving about two feet of space between us. *For about ten minutes or so we both sat there silently.*

There may be no words exchanged, especially when the worker knows that the client's feelings are so powerful that he may want to experience them alone before telling anyone of them, if at all.

Engaging in the other's medium is a way of connecting to others amply illustrated in the "hanging around" of gang workers and researchers interested in entering the lives of groups when these groups are likely to perceive them as alien at the outset. In the following instance, the social worker wants to give Joe some information obtained from the school counselor about returning to school. Joe is playing pinball with three other fellows in the poolroom and is not interested in stopping or in acknowledging the adult who has just entered. The worker knows it is hard for Joe to talk about his expulsion and his future at that moment, and times his approach with this in mind as he joins the group at the pinball machine and plays with them by trying a few games himself.

When I spotted Joe he was horsing around with three other fellows whom I didn't know at the pinball machine. *I went to their machine and watched.* Joe was high scorer up to this point. He played three more rounds. *I waited and watched, and finally took two turns myself while they watched.* Finally, one of the boys took over and Joe gave me a long look. I slowly started out of the poolroom, and Joe followed me.

PROPOSING A MEDIUM PRESUMABLY CONGENIAL TO THE OTHER

To propose a medium presumably congenial to the other is to initiate interaction in a particular activitiy known by the worker to be familiar to the other. Proposing other than verbal interaction media, like engaging in a nonverbal medium, is used to lead to more open communication when verbal overtures do not bring response or when the worker believes they would not. Again, this behavior is desirable if, and only if, its use might increase the comfort of the other.

Proposing a medium presumed to be congenial to the other involves making some assumptions about the other's preferred form of interaction. Sometimes the situation suggests a form of interaction other than words, as for example, taking a walk or playing catch with a child who looks as if talking would not come easily. Or a worker's decision to offer an activity rather than a verbal dialogue might spring from knowledge of age, cultural, or other general characteristics assumed to interest others who seem similar to the person in question. In certain instances an offer of a cup of tea or even of a cigarette might break the ice. At other times it is the worker's knowledge about the interests, skills, or accomplishments of the particular person that leads to a specific suggested form of engagement.

In order to make such assumptions, the social worker must first reach for analogues. To reach for analogues is to ask the question: "What does this remind me of?" The answer is sought from among the paradigms with which the worker is familiar.[16]

By connecting present circumstances with analogues stored in memory, the worker formulates an answer to the professional questions "What should I do?" "How should I do it?" [17] Based on the particular analogue the worker selects, he offers the client a means through which their interaction can begin that will presumably interest rather than offend. Such proposals of congenial formats are aimed to lead to verbal communication and work on the task that connects the worker and client.

In the following illustration the social worker makes inferences about what a teenager would like to do while talking with him after he notes that she wants to talk with him but is uncomfortable with his office arrangement.

Kay walked into the office, looked around at all the desks, and frowned at me. *I suggested that we walk over to the soda machine.*

This example shows the worker deciding upon a form of engagement with a client drawn from generalized knowledge about the likes and dislikes of an age population. To the extent that the worker's knowledge about categories of persons is reliable, he can make such a proposal with confidence. But, as with all categorical knowledge, he must also be prepared for a rejection by any particular individual.

Sometimes, as in the following example, the worker's proposal derives from particular previous experience or knowledge about the individual. Here, the worker knew that Dan liked to play pool and could assume that an offer to play pool with him was a fairly safe suggestion.

I had spoken to Dan, a patient in the hospital, several times in the recreation area. He usually shot pool during our interactions. Today, he was sitting down, hands clasped over his head, just behind the pool table area. *I said, "Hey, want to shoot some pool?"*

The final example of proposing a medium that might be

congenial to the other derives from the exigencies of the moment and the social worker's analytic behavior of reaching for an analogue out of his own past. Finding Ed fighting in a school corridor in front of an excited audience, he stopped the fight by physically forcing the student away from the others. Then he took him by the shoulders and walked with him to get rid of the pent-up energy and excitement. The social worker knew that only physical involvement could begin to deal with the heightened physical excitation of the moment. No amount of words would be adequate to the situation.

After I broke up the fight and the onlookers went to their next class, I noticed that Ed, who had held the other two at bay, was shaking. Remembering my own fights in high school, I thought he might want to talk off some of the left-over feeling, so *I led him into an unoccupied room by the shoulders where we walked in large circles* while we talked.

ATTENDING

To attend is actively to take in diverse communication cues from the other, and to convey to the other that these are being taken in. Hence, attending behavior involves sensory and cognitive processes on the one hand, and interpersonal communication processes on the other hand. Skill in attending refers to the smooth synchronization of sensory, cognitive, and communicative processes used continuously during interaction with others regardless of which individual happens to be speaking at the moment.

In the first place, attending has to do with the processes of perception and selection. In the perception process the social worker receives various verbal and nonverbal stimuli from the client, screened and limited by how much of it he is physiologically able to receive. He then imparts meaning to the messages; that is, he conceptualizes them, through a translation process in the brain which further screens and limits how much of the information is taken in through the grid of the worker's personal/professional frame of reference.[18] Perception, thus is a consequence of this living experience in which the social worker busily receives, screens, and processes the messages communicated, and makes some internal predictions about how the external events are likely to unfold while his response is being organized.[19] Out of all the stimuli, the social worker decides what is the main message and what is simply embellishment or distraction, and gears his attending to encourage expression of the former. In other words, between attending and responding to the information or feeling conveyed by the client, the social worker uses such analytic behaviors in his store of translation processes as searching for key variables, combining variables, and recombining variables, all the while distinguishing and separating his feelings from those of the other, his values from the other's.

To perceive the essence of a situation and to communicate precisely what one intends to communicate with respect to that situation, one must be aware of his own values and biases and in control of his own nonverbal behavior. To refrain from unknowingly communicating those feelings, attitudes, and judgments which belong within the worker rather than between the worker and the other requires a particular vigilance on the part of the worker. This is not to suggest a feeling-less worker nor to propose "scientific objectivity" as the ideal; for the worker who knows his own feelings and can report them as needed when working on a given task [20] is the one who can also encourage the other to know his own feelings as one vital element in meeting problematic situations. Such sensitivity to the other requires an active internal dialogue through which one's own values, biases, and feelings at the moment are known as *one's own,* and controlled in order to maximize perception of the situation and responsiveness to others.

Attending skill appears as skill in looking and listening. While the social worker may remain essentially silent during the attending process, he is nevertheless vigorously engaged in an active internal analysis through which he seeks to answer such questions as: What is the other expressing? What is the other *really* expressing? What is he asking of me? Specifically, the social worker is observing the other—his facial expression, posture, gestures, and other bodily cues—by scanning his face and the rest of his person through a series of short glances or longer, more intense glances when messages deemed particularly important are conveyed. He is simultaneously listening to the words themselves and to the paralinguistic and emotive aspects of speech—tone, cadence, pauses, pitch, and so forth. In short, the worker is following the other.[21] He is following information and he is following feeling.

At the same time, the worker is also providing a series of tiny communication cues to the other, um-hum, head nods, and so forth,[22] that signal such messages as, "Go on," "I am interested in you," "I am interested in what you are saying." Part of attending is control of the worker's own behaviors so that they are congruent with the message of interest and concern that he wants to convey. For it is patently impossible that the client will feel attended to if the worker is busy jotting down notes, or if he gazes out the window, fidgets, yawns, or in other subtle (primarily nonverbal) ways transmits a contrary message.[23] To attend, then, is also to convey poised concern that is mobilized in the service of the other.

In the following episode the social worker reveals her own focus upon attending by the detail with which she describes the communication exchange. It is obvious that this worker regards her own behavior as related to, and possibly responsible for, the client's detailed description of her situation. In this example, the worker's "ooh," head nod, tilt of the head, and smile when she detected a bit of sarcasm, are the tiny microacts through which she conveyed her value of Mrs. F. and encouragement that it would be all right for her to get her complaints off her chest as a prelude to determining just what she wanted the social worker to help with.

Mrs. F. came to talk with me about "everything going wrong in the last couple of days." *I said, "Ooh" and waited.* She continued, "I am married and I have two children, ages five and three. My husband is working as a driver for an electrical company." *I nodded.* "We moved to this Project two months ago," she went on. "And you know how pleasant it is here," she added sarcastically. *I tilted my head a little and smiled.* "Well," she said, "it started with the toilet. Then Billy, he's the older one . . ."

Using the attending skill, the social worker may follow facts or feelings or both. In the example cited, the worker was primarily attending a factual presentation of the problems the client was facing up to the point where a sarcastic tone suggested the deep feelings that accompanied the facts. In the next example, the social worker is attending a flood of feelings expressed by a colleague, a nurse, in a school system. After the nurse is apparently satisfied that the social worker heard her feelings, she moves to present some facts, specific episodes that have given rise to her feelings. In this instance the school nurse is white while the social worker and the students being discussed are black. One can appreciate the strain the social worker must have been under, keeping her own feelings and responses under control as she attended to the other's feelings and biases. Had she not been able to attend to the nurse and really hear her, had she tried to combat these feelings midway through the expression of them, the chances for further work with the nurse would have been diminished.

While talking with the school nurse about the problems of the pregnant girls in the school, she named some students she would like me to work with and went off into a lengthy description of her opinions about the situation. She detailed her disappointment with those who didn't want abortions, her disgust with their attitude about sex, her opinion of their immaturity, their lack of responsibility, and so forth. *I sat quietly and listened and watched* as she talked. She then related an episode in which she chastised one girl with, "Just because you have an abortion doesn't give you a license to engage in sex so freely," and mentioned another who announced in class without any reservation that she was expecting her second child by a second father.

Clearly, this social worker's objectives included hearing out the nurse rather than confronting her opinions and beliefs at that time out of an overreaching desire to make some plan for her own direct involvement with the pregnant students. To reach this end she would have to arrive at a working arrangement with the nurse.

The next example illustrates the social worker attending a student's presentation of his dilemma and at the same time engaging in an internal analytic process to make sense out of the report he is receiving.

Talking with John just after the fight he had at school, I said, "Wow, man, you're hot!" and he launched into a description of why this fight had taken place. *I listened.* From what I could gather this was a gang-related fight. Actually, it was a power-pressure tactic used to recruit him into one of the gangs. He had just been released from the state delinquency institution and thus was a free agent not associated with any gang.

The final example also illustrates the social worker attending to several aspects at once. In this instance, the multiple demand upon the worker is that of attending to the behavior of several other persons in a group at the same time he is talking to one particular person.

In a staff meeting group of eight persons I reminded Dr. G. that he had agreed to distribute the letter to the total staff a week ago. *During this interaction P. was taking notes, and his assistant was frowning. The staff psychiatrist and social services director were looking at P. and the others were waiting* for Dr. G. to respond.

These examples suggest that attending is a complex skill; only on the surface is it simply looking and listening. The worker is taking in cues from the others, and conceptualizing the information he receives. He is concerned about leaving room for the others and needs to hold his own reactions and ideas in momentary check so that the other gets the impression that he is not following the social worker's scenario, but has really a hand in the course of the interaction. He is also concerned about conveying encouragement and warmth to the client through specific microacts, by smiling, absence of idio-syncratic or distracting movements, frequent eye contact, or a bodily lean toward the client (continued positioning).[24]

Chapter 8

Skill in Engaging Feelings

People have feelings about themselves and their plight, about making decisions and taking definitive action. People have feelings about having feelings, and all of these are inextricably bound to definition and accomplishment of the task. If the feelings that surround a description of pressures, an expression of need, and/or a choice of action are not openly engaged, they become obstacles to the work, subtly distorting information sent and received and/or blocking movement toward the stated goal. Witness the advocate whose clients deny him at the point of confrontation with powerful others. Witness the client who cannot even begin to think about changing his painful situation until he is satisfied that the essence of his pain has been communicated. Feelings are potent forces in the lives of people, simultaneously pulling them in different directions, skewing their perceptions, hurting and frightening them. If the work is to be more than illusory, and task accomplishment more than a cherished ideal, then feelings must be engaged.

It should be noted from the outset that feelings are engaged in order to accomplish the task of reducing the external pressures impinging on the client. The feeling-related behaviors are presented prior to the information-related behaviors not because they are more important, but because their use is often necessary before information can be engaged.

Skill in engaging feelings refers to the use of five specific behaviors: (1) reaching for feelings; [1] (2) waiting out feelings; (3) "getting with" feelings; (4) reporting own feelings; and (5) reaching for a feeling link.

REACHING FOR FEELINGS

To reach for feelings is to ask the other if he is experiencing a particular emotion or set of emotions which the situation presumably evokes.[2] This behavior is appropriate if, and only if, one of three conditions obtains: (1) no emotion is expressed; (2) emotion expressed is not congruent with the situation; or (3) emotion is expressed in an elusive form.

Feelings that are frightening, ego-alien, or socially unacceptable are likely to be denied. When such feelings are too potent to be denied, however, their expression may be embedded in a more or less elusive form. Sometimes they are expressed nonverbally, through posture and gesture, space behavior, facial expression, direction of eye gaze, and/or tone of voice. Silence, too, can be an expression of feeling. At other times, feelings are expressed in questions (What's the matter with him?); commands (Don't touch that!); accusations (You think you're better than we are.); judgments (He's handsome.); and sarcastic comments (Another kid; just what I need.). In some instances the feelings may be expressed in an analogy that leaves the speaker room to modify or deny totally the content of his communication should feedback from the receiver indicate a clear and present danger. Under such conditions, the worker reaches for the feelings of the other by putting "into words what he believes to be the precise state of . . . [the other's] . . . inner experience." [3]

In the first example, a woman describes a frustrating situation without expressing emotion. The worker reaches for her feelings by verbalizing what he presumes to be her precise inner experience.

Mrs. B. said that she had to work and leave her baby with a sitter, that she wasn't too sure about the sitter but that she couldn't afford a better one. In a very matter-of-fact manner she said that it's okay, though, because she goes home every chance she gets to see how the baby is doing. *I said that it must be very frustrating always having to worry about the safety of her child and at the same time trying to do a good job at work.* She sighed deeply, gave me a halfway smile, and said that it was running her ragged.

In the second example, the worker reaches for the feelings of a tenant whose facial expression seems incongruent with his verbal message.

Just before the tenants' meeting, Mr. V. told me that the landlord might throw them all out of the building, or get back at them with not enough heat or something like that. He was smiling. *I said, "You're smiling."* He said, "Yeh? Well I'm a little scared. I'm a lot scared. I've got nowhere else to go."

In the third example, the worker reaches for the feelings of a man whose expression of emotion takes a nonverbal form.

Mr. C. came into the Probation Office, walked over to my desk timidly, cleared his throat nervously, and quietly stuttered out "H . . . Hello." I asked him to have a seat, and when he did he was eyeing the room and fumbling for a cigarette and some matches. *I said, "Mr. C., you really look uptight, very uncomfortable."* He said, "Y . . . Yeh, I know I missed two appointments. Are you going to arrest me or something?"

In the fourth example, the worker reaches for the feelings of a young man whose proxemic behavior suggests the presence of emotion. Although the man responds, his feelings remain elusive, so the worker reaches again.

Mr. J. was unusually quiet and had selected a chair far away from everyone else. *I said softly, "Mr. J., you seem very alone today."* He said, quietly and sadly, "Yeh. By myself." *I nodded and said, "You look as though you were very sad."*

In the fifth example, the worker reaches for the feelings of a colleague who uses an analogy to express her reactions.

After a staff meeting in which the psychologist's plan for a new service was turned down, she asked me if I ever thought about how long it takes a spider to spin a web and how fast it can be wiped out of the corner with a dust rag. *I said that it sounded very demoralizing.* She looked at me with a sad expression on her face and nodded.

WAITING OUT FEELINGS

To wait out feelings is to remain silent while the other experiences his own emotions.[4] This behavior is called for when: (1) the worker has just reached for the feelings of the other; (2) the verbal behavior of the other stops abruptly; and/or (3) the nonverbal behavior of the other seems to signal *time out*.[5]

Waiting out feelings is perhaps the hardest behavior to enact, for silence is discomfiting, and there is a natural tendency to fill it with a plethora of words. But people experiencing emotion need room to engage themselves in an internal dialogue through which they can either contact and claim their own feelings, compose themselves in order to project an image of themselves consonant with their inner experience, or both. The worker must contain [6] himself lest he deny the other the right to feel.

In the first example, the worker reaches for feelings and then silently waits them out.

Mrs. M. said she left her husband and two little children. She said she wanted to take the children with her, but didn't have any way to support them. She said she needed a job, that maybe then she could get the children. Her voice was trembling and her eyes filled up. *I said she looked as though she were about to cry.* She denied this, and there was silence. *I waited.* After several silent minutes during which she tilted her head back to keep the tears from running down her face, she sobbed deeply and let the tears run down.

In the second example, the worker waits out the feelings of an elderly man whose verbal communication stops abruptly. The silence that follows is broken by his active claim to the emotion he is experiencing.

"Something has to be done about the situation," said Mr. G. "I'm not worried about the kids breaking into my place. What worries me is . . ." Silence. *I waited.* "I'm afraid to walk outside," he whispered.

In the third example, the worker waits out the feelings of a woman whose nonverbal behavior seems to signal *time out.*

Mrs. S. stated that she didn't want to go to a nursing home because she would not have anything to look forward to but just sitting around getting older. She said that just to know there was housework to do gave her something to look forward to the next day. She closed her eyes, and *both of us were silent for a minute or so.* Then Mrs. S. said, "Everyone needs something to look forward to."

"GETTING WITH" FEELINGS

To "get with" feelings is to indicate to the other that the essence of his inner experience has been communicated. The statement "I understand" will not suffice, for the client has no way of knowing if the worker who says "I understand" actually does understand. Rather, the worker must *demonstrate* his understanding by accurately reflecting [7] the feelings that the client expresses. In order to "get with" feelings, then, the worker must (1) step outside his own frame of reference in order to see the world as his client sees it, and (2) accurately state his own understanding of the client's emotional experience. Only in this way can the worker show the client that he is with him, that he really does understand how it is.

The act of getting with feelings is suitable if, and only if, the other has actually communicated a feeling or set of feelings, and *must* be carried out if the feelings are communicated in response to prior acts of reaching for feelings and/or waiting out feelings.

In the first example, the worker gets with the feelings of the resident supervisor of a children's institution.

After hanging up the phone, Mrs. H. commented that "nobody can do anything by themselves." She told me they constantly bother her. She told me about her many and varied job duties and how tired it all makes her, and how in addition to all that she has to make regular rounds because if she didn't things were likely to fall apart. *I said, "That's exhausting!"*

In the second example, the worker initially waits out feelings. Then, when the feelings are communicated, she gets with them by stating precisely what she understands to be the inner experience of the other.

Mrs. L. was recently admitted to the nursing home. She told me that she had been in the hospital and the doctors made a mistake and told her she was dying of terminal cancer. Her son let her apartment go and sold all her possessions. She looked very sad, and her voice was weak and trembling. *I waited.* After a short silence, Mrs. L. said she felt numb. *I said, "Finding out you were going to live wasn't such good news after all."* She pressed my hand as she nodded and said, "It would almost have been better to die."

REPORTING OWN FEELINGS

To report one's own feelings is to tell the other the precise state of one's own inner experience. This behavior should be used if, and only if, the report may shed light on what the other is feeling, or what is happening in the situation.

Two cautions regarding misuse of this behavior should be noted. First, the worker should not give opinions in the guise of reporting his own feelings. A statement such as "I feel that we're making the decision too quickly," for example, is not a report of feeling. Rather, it is a report of opinion, and is more accurately preceded by "I think"—"I think that we're making the decision too quickly." Second, the worker should not report his own feelings in order to induce the other to act. For example, the statement "I feel uncomfortable when you sit there with your coat on" is more than a report of feelings. It is an effort to get the other to remove his coat. The worker reports his own feelings not to tell others how to behave, but to make his feelings available as information that others can use, if they wish and as they wish, in order to contact their own feelings and/or understand the dynamics of the situation.

In the first example, the worker reports his own feelings to a group of high school students and their parents in order to shed light on what others may be feeling when the atmosphere of the meeting dramatically changes after one student's remark.

The group was engaging in a final rehearsal before the meeting with school administrators. Mr. S. made his extreme demand in a loud voice and Ms. N. qualified it, as planned. Mr. T., who was playing the role of the principal, said that he understood the parents' concern and supported it, but that the parents would have to understand that the schools can't raise a child's God-given intelligence level. Suddenly R. shouted, "You racist bastard!" In the moments that followed there was some laughter and a lot of chattering. The role play stopped, and although both students and parents continued to discuss the impending meeting, the interaction was very strained. *I said that I felt tense and wondered if anyone else felt that way too.*

In the second example, the worker reports his feeling of defensiveness to a group of staff people in order to shed light on what may be happening in the situation, i.e., an attack.

Following my comment that sometimes we see crazy behavior because this is a mental hospital and we expect and look for crazy behavior, one of the psychiatrists asked me if I knew much about pathology. I felt my muscles tense up and I said, *"Wow! I'm starting to feel defensive."*

REACHING FOR A FEELING LINK

To reach for a feeling link is to ask others to connect with a feeling being expressed. This behavior is appropriate if, and only if, two conditions obtain: a feeling is expressed, and more than two persons are present. In situations that meet the first condition but do not meet the second condition, the proper behavior is to get with feelings.

In situations that meet both conditions, however, the worker is not the only person who can demonstrate to another that his inner experience has been understood. Every person present at the time a feeling is expressed has the potential to empathize and to communicate that empathy, and the worker reaches for a feeling link in order to realize that potential. This is consistent with the principle of maximizing environmental supports. That is to say, when others are present, the worker does not occupy the central position by getting with feelings. Rather, he reaches for a feeling link.

In the first example, the worker reaches for a feeling link between a troubled junior high school boy and some of his classmates.

D. asked the other boys if anyone could crash him that night (let him sleep at their house). T. said, "A-gain, man?" D. flashed his eyes at T., then retreated to a corner and stared at the floor. I said that D. looked pretty upset. T. said he couldn't help that, that his mother told him if he brought D. home one more time this week she'd throw them both out in the street. R. asked D. what was the matter with his own house. D. didn't answer. T. played with his shoelace and mumbled that D. can't go home when his mother's working. D. shouted at T. that T. better shut up or he'd waste him. There was some silence during which a few of the boys glanced at D., and T. kept playing with his shoelace. *I asked if anyone could imagine what D. must be feeling.* T. nodded. E. said that D. must be mad. T. said, "And embarrassed." D. looked over at the group, then sat down where he was. R. asked D. if he wanted to go home with him. D. moved a little closer to the group and asked R. if he had to ask his mother. "She don't care," R. answered, and moved closer to D. E. said if D. wanted, he could stay with him next time. T. said that by next week D. could probably stay with him a couple of nights again, too.

In the second example, the worker reaches for a feeling link between an employee resisting peer pressure and his pressuring peers.

During a meeting of Housing Authority employees outraged by the recent repressive edicts from administration, there was talk of joining the tenants' protest march organized by some members of the Residents Advisory Board. The idea quickly gathered support, even from some of those who initially indicated that, in their opinion, such an action would not accomplish anything. Mr. F., however, continued to oppose the move, and when someone accused him of being afraid to stand up, he shouted, "You're damn right, I am. I've got a family to support and I need my job." *I asked if any one else was feeling some of what Mr. F. was feeling.* Mrs. J. said that she was a little afraid, too. Several others nodded. Mr. S. said that he only had himself to worry about, but that if he had a family, he would probably be afraid, too. Mrs. O. asked if the Housing Authority could really fire them for doing something like that.

Chapter 9

Skill in Engaging Information

Information is a resource that reduces uncertainty by giving form or character to a situation or event. That is to say, a situation or event is knowable to the extent that information pertinent to that situation or event can be generated, collected, manipulated, and reconstructed. And to the extent that a situation or event is known, there can be precision in task definition and determination of action to accomplish the task defined. It follows that engaging information is central to social work practice.

Skill in engaging information is the use of eight specific behaviors: (1) reaching for information; (2) partializing; (3) giving information; (4) running out alternatives; (5) pointing out possible consequences; (6) recasting problems; (7) connecting discrete events; and (8) summarizing.

REACHING FOR INFORMATION

To reach for information is to ask the other for facts, opinions, values and/or judgments that increase knowledge of a situation or event. This behavior is proper if, and only if, the nature of the situation or event is uncertain. Hence, the worker's efforts to elicit information he already knows in order to teach or otherwise influence the other (the Socratic method) are precluded.

When the nature of the situation or event is uncertain, reaching for information takes two different forms: (1) open-ended questions (What happened?) and (2) close-ended questions (Have you told John?). Open-ended questions are suitable for exploratory purposes, while close-ended questions are used to focus attention on key issues [1] and clarify information provided.

In the first two examples, the workers use open-ended questions for exploratory purposes.

K. said that the atmosphere was different today. *I asked him if he could talk a little more about that.*

L. said that he'd like to punch the teacher in the mouth. He said the teacher was always picking on him and he was tired of it. *I asked L. to tell me some more about the conflict between him and the teacher.*

In the third example, the worker uses a close-ended question in order to focus attention on a key issue.

Mrs. S. described their continual conflict with the landlord over such things as the water being off for days so that even the toilet wouldn't flush, or the heat or the gas being off. She said that when they complain, he tells them they can move if they don't like it, but where can they move to? They don't know anywhere it would be better. Mr. S. said that now it's the heat that's off, and that when he told the landlord they had no heat, the landlord said that they did have heat. Mr. S. said he pushed him a little, that he wanted to flatten him, but he only pushed him a little. Mrs. S. said that the landlord frequently makes remarks about "niggers" and "spics" not deserving to get anything. *I asked them if they'd want to move if there was a better place around.* They both said yes.

In the fourth example, the worker uses a close-ended question in order to clarify the information provided.

Mr. B. took off his hat and sat down in the folding chair near my desk. He leaned back and sighed, "Those sons of bitches. They ain't no damned good." *I said, "Who?"* He said, "My kids."

PARTIALIZING

To partialize is to divide a problem into smaller, more manageable parts. This behavior is appropriate when the pressures that the client describes are many and complex or when simultaneous concern with many aspects of a problem confounds the work.

People confronted by large and complex problems tend to feel them as total life experiences that cannot be altered. Such statements as "everything is wrong" and "there is nothing that can be done" reflect a felt totality that both overwhelms and immobilizes. Likewise, the many complex issues that can arise in the course of selecting action to accomplish a task can diffuse energy and retard progress toward the goal. By partializing, the worker separates the overwhelming whole into a series of manageable units.

In the first example, the worker gets with the felt totality that the client's initial statement reflects, reaches for information with an open-ended question in order to explore the situation, and then partializes the pressures impinging on the client into two separate units for action.

Mr. B. said that everything suddenly collapsed. *"Wow!" I said. "What happened?"* He said that two months ago he was working and looking forward to retiring so he and his wife could do some of the things they always talked about doing. Now nothing. He went on to describe his wife's death and his futile efforts to keep the company from retiring him. He said there was nothing to do, nobody to be with, and no reason to get up in the morning. After we talked about how lonely he feels *I said that two things seemed to be making him feel lonely: not having anything to do since he didn't have a job, and not having anyone to be with since his wife died.*

In the second example, the worker partializes when decision-making is confounded by simultaneous concern with many aspects of a problem.

The first suggestion regarding how to get everyone to the rally involved chartering a bus. Mrs. A. said that not everyone could afford to kick in to cover the cost of the bus, and Mr. L. asked what about people who couldn't get there on time because of things that come up, like with the kids. Mrs. D. said that maybe car pools would be better, but Mrs. J. said they don't have enough cars between them and there was gas money to consider. A couple of people expressed the feeling that it was useless to go on discussing it, that there was no way for them to get to the rally. *I said that maybe they were getting bogged down because they were trying to work on three things at once: first there was the question of how to get to the rally; then there was the question of how to pay for it; and there was a third question about a departure time that would be convenient for everyone.*

GIVING INFORMATION

To give information is to offer the other person facts, opinions, and/or ideas that may increase his knowledge of a situation or event. This behavior is appropriate if, and only if, the information is relevant to the task at hand, and not already available to the other.

As indicated earlier, information is a resource. Given the relationship between possession of resources and possession of power, when the worker gives the client information he increases the client's power to exercise some measure of control over his own experiences. But this proposition holds only when the information is both relevant and not previously available to the client. Giving information that is not relevant diverts attention from the situation at hand, and giving information that the client already possesses tends to influence his decision by emphasizing particular facts and/or opinions as opposed to all possible facts and/or opinions.[2] In both instances, the client's power to make choices in accord with his own definition of his best interest in a particular situation is decreased rather than increased.

A third, related caution that should be noted here involves information of the idea or opinion type. Ideas and opinions that are presented as established "truths" distort and manipulate, hence decrease the client's power to determine the course of his life. For the client's power to be increased by the ideas and opinions that the worker gives, the worker must present them as *his own*. That is to say, the worker must explicitly indicate that his ideas and opinions represent but one fragment of available social experience.[3]

In the first example, the worker gives information to a man who recently moved from the home of a relative to a nursing home.

"They still didn't send my social security check here and they won't give me any spending money," he continued. "They tell me I'm always complaining and I'm not; I just want what's mine. But how do I get it?" *I told him about filing a change of address card with the post office and letting the social security office know he had a new address.*

In the second example, the worker gives factual information and then information of the opinion type. In the latter instance, she explicitly defines the opinion as her own.

Mrs. H. asked me how to get to Third and Arcady and *I told her which bus went there.* She told me she didn't have money for the bus, that she wanted to know how to walk there. *I told her how and then said that I thought it was dangerous for a woman to walk there alone at night, that other people might not agree, but that it seemed dangerous to me.*

RUNNING OUT ALTERNATIVES

To run out alternatives is to list possible courses of action for the other to consider. This behavior is a special case of giving information, and as such it is subject to the same conditions. Use of the behavior is illustrated in the following example where the worker initially gives information and then suggests two alternatives.

When I went into the day room to see Mrs. R. she was holding a magazine up in front of her face and would not look at me. I waited several minutes and then said, *"Mrs. R., you don't have to talk to me if you don't want to; it's okay with me if you'd rather look at your magazine and talk to me another time, or do you want to talk to me now?"* She said quietly, not looking up, "Look at the magazine."

POINTING OUT POSSIBLE CONSEQUENCES

To point out possible consequences is to indicate the possible outcomes of alternatives under consideration by the other; hence this behavior is frequently, though not always, used in combination with running out alternatives. Like running out alternatives, pointing out possible consequences is also a special case of giving information and is therefore also subject to the conditions for giving information.

In the first example, the worker reaches for information and then points out a possible consequence.

Members of the Mental Patients' Civil Rights Organization on the adolescent ward were talking about getting B. to join when B. walked in and sat down. After some brief, welcoming exchanges *I asked B. if she had permission to be here.* She said no, that she snuck away from O. T. in order to come. *I told her that if the O. T.s discovered her absence she could lose her grounds privileges for a week, which would keep her from attending the next two meetings.*

In the second example, the worker runs out three alternatives and points to a possible consequence.

Mr. D. said that he couldn't bear the thought of spending the rest of his life in a nursing home. He said that there was nothing to do there, and that most of the residents were senile that he feared for his own sanity. After much discussion during which he expressed a lot of feeling and I tried to get with the feelings he was expressing, he asked me what he could do. *I said that there were at least three alternatives we could explore. There are other nursing homes; there are boarding homes; and possibly living with a relative if that was okay with him and with the relative.* He said that relatives were out, but that a boarding home or even a different nursing home might make a difference. He said it certainly couldn't be worse than it was here. *I said that other nursing homes might also have residents who were senile.* He nodded and said he could take that if there were something to do, or if there were nothing to do but not all that senility—he just couldn't take both at the same time.

RECASTING PROBLEMS

To recast a problem is to provide a different vantage point for thinking about troublesome issues,[4] thereby shifting and/or increasing the range of alternative actions for dealing with them. Use of the behavior is illustrated in the following example.

One of the senior citizens began writing a list of those present and their phone numbers. Several people had difficulty recalling their numbers and seemed embarrassed by it. Someone said, "That's what happens when you get old." Others agreed. *I said that sometimes I have trouble thinking of my phone number simply because I never call myself on the phone.* One woman said that she remembers other people's numbers but not her own. Another woman said they should be careful before they blame everything on being old. Several people helped each other by reminding them of their phone numbers.

CONNECTING DISCRETE EVENTS

To connect discrete events is to ask the other if two or more separate occurrences may be related. This behavior is suitable when the client does not connect the events he describes if, and only if, (1) the worker infers a connection, and (2) connecting the events puts a different perspective on the client's plight. With respect to the latter condition, connecting discrete events is a special case of recasting problems.

The number and complexity of interaction sequences in the various systems of demand and relationship in which persons live their daily lives can obscure connections between events so that each seems self-contained and wholly separate from the other. Similarly, political and economic events can seem unrelated to interpersonal relations and/or inner experiences. By connecting apparently discrete events, problems can be understood from new perspectives; pressures can be seen to emanate from different sources; and new actions to lessen the pressures can be taken.

In the following example, the worker connects a client's budgeting problem to increased prices, thereby shifting the presumed source of the problem, hence the locus for change efforts, from the client to the economic arrangements.

Mrs. S. said she was slipping, that she used to be able to make ends meet, but that lately she winds up on Thursday with more mouths than food. She said she needed help managing her money. As we continued to talk, Mrs. S. told me she cleans for three people and that she has been with those people for years. She said she gets $10 and bus fare per day. She knew that food prices had increased, but she didn't connect high prices to her fixed income and "budgeting problem." *I asked her if they might be related,* and she looked puzzled for a few seconds then asked me if it was possible that it wasn't her fault. I nodded. She said she figured she always made it on the money she got and that if she wasn't making it now it had to be her. We talked about the minimum wage law.

In the second example, the worker connects a young veteran's decision to rejoin the army to difficulties he is experiencing with his parents. With this new perspective, the veteran makes a different plan for himself.

Mr. A. had been out of the army for three weeks when he told me he was foolish to get out, that the regimentation he hated wasn't all that bad, that there were lots of good parts. (Two weeks ago when he came to the VA for information regarding education benefits he said he hated the army, that it interrupted his education and his love life, that the rules were inhuman, and that a guy could get killed there. He said he was going to let his mother feed him and go back to college.) I asked him if he had talked to his parents about reenlisting, and he said he can't talk to them about anything, that he never could, and that they are always on his back about something so trivial it's even more ludicrous. "But that's the way they are," he said, "so it doesn't bother me." *I asked him if his parents being on his back could have anything to do with making the army look good to him.* "Maybe," he said. "It's the only way I can get out of their house." I asked him if he wanted to think about other ways to get out of his parents' house besides going back in the army, and he said that if there were any possible way, he'd never go near the army or his parents again.

SUMMARIZING

To summarize is to state the essence of a particular discussion or series of discussions, action or series of actions. This behavior is indicated whenever next steps are to be determined. It should be used at the end of a transaction in order to specify the issue for a future interaction and/or the actions to be taken in the interim. It should be used at the beginning of a transaction in order to set the focus. And it *must* be used before the terms of a service contract are agreed upon by both worker and client. Summarizing answers the question: Where have we been? Therefore its use should precede efforts to answer the question: Where do we go from here?

In the following example, the worker summarizes at the end of a transaction. The terms of the service contract are made explicit, and both worker and client agree to them.

At the end of the meeting *I said, "Now, where are we? You said you're clean and you want to stay that way, but that's not what you want to talk to me about. The thing you want to talk to me about is getting a job. We marked off some possibilities in the newspaper, and you said you are going to go to those places this week. Are we together so far?"* He said, "Yep." I said, "As for my part in it, I'm going to check further with the job unit here. Okay?" He said that was good. *"And we agreed to meet again next Tuesday at 1:30 to see where we are with the job hunting, right?"* I checked. "Right," he answered. We shook hands and he left.

Chapter 10

Skill in Managing Interaction and Engaging Barriers

For human communication to take place, someone has to send a message and someone has to receive it. The sender has to encode the message in symbols, like words and facial expressions, that the receiver can observe. The receiver has to observe the symbols and decode, or interpret, them. Because this is a complex process, there are many spots where it can bog down, obstruct, or completely block communication. If the sender uses symbols that do not accurately portray the message he wants to send, for example, or if his code is not precise, or if it is too subtle for the receiver to observe, then the message received may be wholly different from the message the sender intended to send. Similarly, if the receiver observes some but not all of the symbols, or if he misinterprets the symbols, then he will receive a distorted version of the sender's message. When this happens, people wind up talking to each other without communicating, and each can leave the interaction with a different version of what he is sure they jointly planned.

MANAGING INTERACTION

To prevent communication problems from blocking work on the client task, the social worker needs skill in managing interaction. He needs a repertoire of behaviors for increasing accuracy in expression and recognition of meaning and, for directing messages to the people for whom they are intended. Whenever messages are unclear or misdirected, the worker must interupt the communication process and use his skill in managing interaction to correct it.

Underlying the use of this skill is an assumption that it is hard for people to talk to each other with purpose and with affect. People tend to protect themselves by not saying all they mean or wish to say, by not revealing their feelings, or by not telling the proper person what they think or feel, because this is often too difficult. Individuals avoid direct communication in order to avoid being vulnerable. Sometimes miscommunication stems from the parties' being afraid to hurt others, or to be hurt by others; sometimes from being unsure themselves of what they mean to convey; and sometimes from the problems of the differences in meaning drawn from words as a result of the limitations of words or the cultural and/or experiential variables in the lives of the persons involved. Communication may be obscured by momentary obstacles, such as preoccupation with other ideas, distraction, charisma of the speaker; by environmental obstacles, such as the setting, numbers of people involved; or by interpersonal obstacles, such as, status relationships, hidden agendas, and vested interests. Common communication problems stem from too much or too little information, arriving too early or too late, with irrelevant affect, in an "improper" place. Any one of these events needs correction in order for the message to be heard and understood.

The social worker's attention in managing interaction is di-

rected toward making the communication a two-way inter-
change. In other words, it becomes important that the intended
message is sent and received. On the one hand, the social worker
focuses upon distortions of meaning; on the other hand, he
focuses upon the information the communicator gives away
about himself while he is communicating. For interactional
behavior is at one and the same time communicative and expressive. That is to say, as an individual conveys what he aims
to get across to the other person, he is also conveying information about himself, his physiological state, his felt status, his
estimate of the other, his attitude, his background.[1] He com-
municates both a particular message content and an image of
himself, asking something of the other: agree with me; like me;
don't embarrass me.

That interaction proceeds as smoothly as it does is a result
of tradition (which prescribes what is "proper" as to content,
style, and action), personal determinants (which prescribe
what the individual wants to say and can say), and social factors
(which prescribe where the individuals are in relation to each
other and to the context). Thus, norms, habits, and roles provide expectations bounding interpersonal interactions to a certain extent. That is, they set patterns for the communicative
flow that takes some of the guesswork out of the exchange.
Nevertheless, even patterned interaction needs occasional interruption in order to keep it on course.

Skill in managing interaction refers to the use of six specific
behaviors: (1) checking out inferences and assumptions; (2)
giving feedback; (3) amplifying subtle messages; (4) toning
down strong messages; (5) redirecting a message; and (6)
talking in the idiom of the other.

CHECKING OUT INFERENCES AND ASSUMPTIONS

To check out an inference or assumption is to ask if a certain
thought, feeling, belief, or interpretation is valid for the other

person in a particular situation. In other words, the social worker checks out inferences and assumptions to validate whether or not his assumed meaning is the intended meaning. Since he knows his own frame of reference is capable of obscuring the other's real meaning, the social worker uses this behavior as a corrective measure to answer his persistent question, "What is going on right now?" By checking out with the other whether or not his interpretation is accurate, the social worker is asking for confirmation or disconfirmation of this judgment.

Distortions arising from the limitation imposed by the frame of reference of each individual affect all communication. Each person's communication flows through his own screen, and then through the other's screen, before it is received. The response is to what one hears rather than to what might have been intended. And this reponse also goes through one's own screen, and then through the other's screen, before it is interpreted. Since two screening frames of reference in a two-person exchange, and many screening frames of reference in a group interaction, must operate every time messages are sent and received, it is obvious that many additions, subtractions, and distortions of information must occur according to the particular screens of the individuals and the modes used to convey the messages—the verbal mode, the many channels of the nonverbal mode, and the symbolic mode (clothing, hair style, jewelry).

Distortions of communication also arise from the imprecision of language itself as an instrument for conveying experience, and from the haphazard, almost automatic way it is often used—as if it were clear. All language exchange is incomplete and needs clarifying and qualifying so that it makes sense to the other person. And yet, it is rarely deliberately viewed as the vague, spotty, shorthand it is, filled with half statements and gaps or sometimes only looks and pauses, (well, *you* know . . .

it's obvious), and sometimes overgeneral (*everyone* should know *this;* or *this* is how *it* is). The meaning is obscure or masked and needs deciphering.

The same word can be a symbol for entirely different items in a denotative sense: "rap" can mean hitting someone, while "rapping with" (sometimes contracted to simply "rapping") refers to talking with someone. At the same time, a word can suggest various ideas in a connotative sense: (to rap is pleasant; to rap hurts, to take the rap is unfair; blacks take more raps than whites). Not only can a word mean many different things or suggest and conjure up many different images, but there may be no words in the language, or in the vocabulary of the client, to describe a given thought or feeling. The language one uses not only reflects how one thinks about the world, but shapes the possibilities of world view and possible actions.[2] For example, dichotomies (things *are* black or white, good or bad) provided by the language makes persons think and act as if life were a series of either/or's. And the problem of overgeneralizing, blanketing in many different things in one fell swoop which then must be sorted out, further distorts communicative intent (e.g., this *always* happens to me). Yet, as Satir suggests, generalizations, though dangerous, are indispensable, for they provide shortcuts to organize experience, enable the person to talk about many different observations at once, and avoid the necessity of evaluating every new event afresh.[3] Verbal exchanges are further cluttered by jargon, clichés, and special vocabularies that are often meaningless to those not familiar with the special code (e.g., This is a multi-service agency . . .).

The social worker must continuously check out his inferences and assumptions to prevent frame-of-reference and/or semantic distortions from shaping his responses, because he is neither a fortuneteller nor an ESP expert. As the following illustration reveals, the social worker must ask questions and make statements to insure that the intended meaning is communicated in the two-way exchange.

Student: *"You* know what I mean . . . the teacher picks on me."
I responded, *"You mean, because you are black?"* Student, "Yeh."
I continued, *"And because I'm black, too, you think I can know
what's happening to you in the classroom."*

In the second example, the social worker points out his inference drawn from the student's posture and eye gaze.

The worker was sitting with Bill, who seemed to be struggling to say something but then hung his head and stared at the floor. I said, *"You look as if you have something to say but can't."* He sat up and said, "You help people with their problems, right?" I answered, *"Right, I help people with their problems. You want me to help you?"* He nodded his head "yes." I nodded also, saying, "Yeah."

Here, the social worker also used a different but related behavior required in instances demanding validation of meaning. That is, he gave feedback: "Right, I help people with their problems."

GIVING FEEDBACK

To give feedback is to repeat the essence of what the other has said and to ask if the meaning received was, in fact, the intended meaning. Giving feedback is used if, and only if, one of the two following conditions are met: (1) the message received was not clear; or (2) the message was clear, but was stereotypic or banal.

Feedback is necessary to expose distortions in the specific content of a message. That is to say, a message may have come across garbled, vague, in unfamiliar words, or in incomprehensible circuituousness. In such instances, the social worker may paraphrase what he thought he heard by stating in his own words what the other's remark conveyed to him. The paraphrase is an at-the-moment, precise, descriptive statement or question that aims to clarify the communication by involving the other in actively listening to the receiver's version of what he said. This version is then either confirmed or rejected as to its accuracy with respect to the meaning intended; and if rejected, the other can then correct his statement or otherwise adjust his presentation to be more accurate.

At times, the social worker may simply state, "I do not understand what you said," and leave it up to the other to restate his message differently. Or the worker can seek more information or clarification through a quizzical look that signals "What do you mean?" These acts are considered as another behavior, reaching for information, rather than giving feedback. The social worker also gives feedback in relation to the expressive portion of the communication rather than only the specific content of the message. This verbal summation of what the other is projecting with words or emotional overtones conveyed verbally and nonverbally is considered herein as a different behavior, reaching for feelings (You told me about yesterday's fight and you look worried). Giving feedback, as isolated from other related skill components, is justified as separate from other feedback behaviors used by the worker through its focus upon the process rather than the content of the exchange. The other acts (reaching for information or feeling) aim directly at fact or feeling as content which is then pursued further.

In other instances, feedback is given to call attention to what has just been said in order to provide the speaker with an opportunity to decide if he wants this message to stand. As an example of this use, consider:

"All students are radicals." *I answered, "You mean to tell me every student is radical?"* He then said, "No, not *every* student, but some that I have met are."

Giving feedback in precise, concise, verbal form helps the sender of the message to make corrections so that his next message may be more on target. This is done by reintroducing a part of his message as new information with a direct or implied qualification that this is how his message was received.

The concept of feedback, drawn from engineering and cybernetics,[4] has been applied to human functioning and communication. Feedback is a control mechanism used at a physiological level to maintain many homeostatic processes (blood pressure, heart rate) as well as at the more voluntary levels (posture adjustment, voice volume) through which the individual informs himself in order to keep in tune with his environment. Giving feedback asks the other to be more clear, either to stay on course or to increase his deviation from the ordinary and understood; that is, to break out of his frame of reference or stereotypes and think more expansively.

In the following example, the social worker gives feedback by paraphrasing a long discussion, particularly emphasizing two points of the client's narrative to check on the accuracy of the meaning received.

Mr. R. said that he had tried to apply for several jobs for which he was qualified and that several persons in the offices just looked at him and put his application somewhere and never called him to tell him whether there was a job, which made him angry. *I asked, "You mean you went to many places to find a job, were ignored, and think they are prejudiced?"* "That's right!" he answered.

The next example shows a communication exchange which was clear enough but seemed too total and overgeneral to the worker, who restated what she had heard in order to allow the student, further to qualify her remarks if she wanted to.

I was discussing with J. her experiences as an aide in the hospital, a part of her work assignment connected with T. High School. I told her the supervisor had reported that she was often late to work and not serious in her duties. J. said, "Mrs. L. never works with the students but expects them to be interested because she is a workhorse." *I said, "You say she works hard but shows no interest in showing any students how to work?"* "No, she takes time with some but not with me."

AMPLIFYING SUBTLE MESSAGES

To amplify a subtle message is to call attention to unnoticed communicative behavior—words, tone of voice, facial expressions—by verbalizing it.[5] The social worker amplifies a subtle message if, and only if, the following three conditions obtain: (1) more than two persons are present; (2) one person's behavior is incongruous with the situation (everyone is laughing but one person is silent and stares at the floor); and (3) others present do not seem to notice the behavior. When other persons are not present, the social worker cannot use this behavior, for he alone (the only person present) has noticed the behavior. Hence it is not subtle for him. Should he call attention to it, he is reaching for feelings, not amplifying a subtle message.

Subtle messages inhere in such aspects of behavior as rapidity of speech, loudness, pitch, speech errors or pauses, timing, and sarcasm (a special instance where inconsistent combinations of verbal and nonverbal cues convey feelings in a faint way). Subtle messages may also be communicated through posture, gesture, facial expression, or eye movements.[6] Underlying the behavior, amplifying subtle messages, is the social worker's recognition that when more than one person is involved in discussion with him, it is difficult and often awkward for the parties to take turns and speak in an orderly sequence. Often several persons would like to express themselves at once; usually the loudest or more persistent is successful in monopolizing the discussion while the others are forced to live with their own reactions, but not verbally express them. Many subtle messages are missed by the parties in their eagerness to have their say. Many are missed by the social worker because it is difficult to attend to several persons' cues at the same time. Furthermore, messages are sometimes sent through subtle ways because it is hard to stand against others and differ with a dominant opinion, because it is hard to express feelings, and because some individuals are not so vocal as others. For these and other reasons, the social worker must busily scan the cues sent simultaneously by all parties in the interaction, and point out certain discrepancies as he sees and hears them, so that these may gain an audience.

In all communication, messages are continuously being sent at two levels: (1) the literal, content level; and (2) the meta-communication level (messages about how the specific content should be taken).[7] Metacommunication messages, often conveyed through subtle means, may signal attitudes about the message (take this seriously; I'm really kidding), attitudes about one's self (I am bored; I feel ignored), or attitudes about the others (they don't care about me; I am better than they are). By attending to both communication levels, the social worker is attending to two aspects of the message: (1) what the actual statement is, and (2) what is being asked of the other (agree with me, believe me). And by noticing the expressive behavior of those persons other than the ones who might be holding forth verbally at a given time, the worker expands the possibilities for others to join the exchange.

In the following example, the social worker amplifies Mr. H.'s messages (head shaking and muttering) which were subtle and unnoticed by the others.

I made a home visit to see Mr. H., a blind, sixty-eight-year-old veteran, who lives with his daughter and son-in-law. The three of them met with me in the living room. All were speaking at the same time, trying to get my attention. Mr. H. was the least successful and began shaking his head and muttering. *I said, "Mr. H. seems to want to get in on this."* The other two stopped and looked at him.

In the next example, the worker uses this behavior in a group situation when he notices Miss. R.'s foot and hand movements.

Mr. C. was talking to the group and lecturing that they shouldn't expect the worker to push them along; they should cooperate and not act like ostriches, putting their heads in the ground. I noticed Miss R., who was sitting next to me shuffling her feet and twisting her handkerchief for some minutes. *I announced to the group, "Miss R. looks as if she has something to say."* All eyes turned to her. Miss R. then said that she agreed with Mr. C.'s point, smiled, and pulled her chair closer to the table.

The following illustration again shows the social worker noticing subtle cues (closed eyes and slight smile) and calling the group's attention to them.

During one segment of the employee committee meeting, grievances to be presented to the agency administrator were being discussed. All grievances were being given cursory examination and added to the list. Mrs. C. was sitting opposite me with her eyes closed and a slight smile on her lips, *I said, "Mrs. C. is sitting here smiling."* Miss J. said, "What are you thinking, Louise?" Miss C. hesitated a moment and then said, "This is ridiculous; if we present all these grievances at once, no one will listen to us." Other members supported her position and a discussion of her motion ensued.

In the next two examples group members are struggling to express feelings. Unpleasant feelings are particularly hard to volunteer. In the first instance, the worker points out an uncomfortable look, while in the second instance a frown is the key to interrupting the process to amplify one person's subtle message.

At a meeting in the senior citizens building at the housing project to discuss specific instances of inadequate security, I noticed Mrs. O. sitting by herself and looking uncomfortable. She was wringing her hands. *I said that Mrs. O. looked uncomfortable.* A couple of people asked her what was wrong, and she said that she came to the meeting because Mrs. M. asked her to, but that she's seventy-five years old and she doesn't want the manager to think she's a troublemaker and lose her apartment.

Mr. D. said the group needed a rule about how long anyone could talk. He said that nobody should talk for more than a minute because some of them would get started about their aches and pains and use up all the time. Someone else said they shouldn't talk about sickness. A few people agreed. Mr. G. was frowning during the entire interaction. *I said, "Mr. G. is frowning."* Several group members turned to Mr. G. and someone asked him what was the matter. He said that sickness was one of the big problems when you're old and it should be talked about here. He said that if they couldn't talk about it to each other, who could they talk to about it? There was lots of agreement.

TONING DOWN STRONG MESSAGES

To tone down a strong message is to verbalize the essence of a highly affective message (shouts, punches, glares) so that the strength of the affect is reduced and the message can be "heard." [8] Strong messages should be toned down if, and only if, there is indication that the others cannot deal with the messages at the intensity or pitch at which they are expressed. That is to say, this specified behavior does not give the social worker license to tone down loud talking or loud actions if the persons involved are used to expressing themselves in such ways. For one is not concerned here with decorum, politeness, civility, or "adult ways of expressing anger." Boys often express all kinds of feeling physically and *can handle this.* Likewise, family members often shout at each other and are quite able to bear each other's anger. Nor is concern for the worker's personal comfort—quiet or orderliness—justification for the act. The worker moves in to the interaction and asks by words or actions that the message be toned down when he notices the others cannot deal with it in its present form. By reducing the affect, the worker makes the situation less terrible and threatening for the one who is the object of the affect, and provides more room for a response from him.

In the following example, the social worker with a senior citizens group in a housing project tones down the message by mentioning that the total group is staring at one member.

While Miss A. was opening the meeting with a prayer, Mrs. S. began to laugh. Miss A. stopped her prayer and, along with the other group members, turned her attention to the laughing Mrs. S. The faces of the group members became rigid with a collective look of anger as they silently focused their eyes on Mrs. S. The group sat silently looking at Mrs. S. who had stopped laughing. The silence lasted about fifteen seconds. Then Miss A., looking straight at Mrs. S., said, "If you laugh once more when God's words are spoken in this group, you will no longer be a member of this group." Still looking at Mrs. S., the others in the group nodded in approval. *I said, Mrs. S. the group is pretty angry at you.*"

It should be noted that this behavior requires the worker to repeat what the group is expressing, using words rather than affect. If the worker had directed her comments to elicit a response from Mrs. S. at that moment ("Mrs. S. you look upset at what the group members said") this would *not* be toning down a strong message. Rather she would be reaching for feelings.

REDIRECTING A MESSAGE

To redirect a message [9] is to ask an individual whose message is intended for another to direct his statement or feeling to that person, whether that person is present or not. This behavior is used if, and only if, one of two conditions obtains: (1) the person directs his message to the worker or other(s) in the situation while the party for whom the message is intended is there hearing it; or (2) the person gives the worker a message intended for someone who is not present.

An assumption underlying the use of this behavior is that people are able to manage their own affairs even though it is difficult and uncomfortable to do so at times. In much the same way as the social worker gives his attention to helping the client take responsibility for making his direct communication as clear and congruent as possible, so does he show the other how ineffective his expression of fact, opinion, or feeling is if it is directed at the wrong target. Misplaced, behind-the-back messages may bring other satisfactions to the sender (relief from pent-up feelings, revenge through influencing others, sympathy from others), but they do nothing toward clearing the air. Worse, they may generate many half truths and increase misinformation now possessed by others beyond the parties involved, and they may dissipate the energy from where the real work lies.

By redirecting messages where they are intended, the social worker is also conveying his own metamessage to the others about the kind of help he offers. That is, he will do what he can to open up lines of communication that have become clogged; he will not get into one side of a problem and then become a messenger who carries the information back and forth between the others. Often persons appeal to the worker, the wrong target for the message, to use his sanction as added power against the other person. Such approaches to settling difficulties may have worked in the past ("Mommy, Johnny is picking on me!").[10] If the social worker falls into such a trap, his metamessage to the client is something like, "Yes, I *do* know better than you what you can say and do. Yes, I will take care of you."

In redirecting the message, the social worker must be careful through tone of voice, facial expression, and words to make this move something other than a put-down or turn-off of the other. That is to say, the worker withholds his involvement *not* because he does not care, but because he cares so much that the client take his difficulty to the proper place where he may get results. It is easier for the social worker to redirect matters of information than feeling issues ("You should be asking Miss. T.; she is the one who can tell you") because it is obvious that the worker may not have the information, and may not be able to implement the request.

Matters of feeling are much more seductive; for the worker might secretly want to counsel and advise the other in his interpersonal behavior. Or he might use such opportunities to gather more information for his own use at some future time. For example, take an instance in which a group member complains to the worker after the meeting about how ineffective the president was. If the worker becomes involved in exploring this, or influencing the complaining member in any direction, he does so only out of such motives as curiosity about how others think the meeting went, or need to protect (or undermine) the president. To affect the course of future meetings, the worker must direct such a reaction back to the person(s) involved—either the president or, better, the total group.

In the following example, the social worker avoids what might be viewed as a handle to get into a mother's feelings about her mothering by directing her question to a future discussion with her children.

I was talking with the mother of one of the fifth-grade children. She told me how busy she was because she worked and was also involved in a number of parent groups. She then said, "I wonder if my not being at home more bothers the children." *I replied, "Did you ever ask your children how they feel about it?"*

In the next example, with a husband and wife, the worker redirects the husband's message and thus avoids placing herself between the two, who must work on their own difficulties.

Mrs. J. told her husband that he doesn't care about her, that if he did he wouldn't run around with all those other girls. Mr. J. leaned toward me and said in a high-pitched voice that he loved his wife and that the other girls don't mean anything to him. *I told him that he should be telling that to Mrs. J.; for she is the one who feels he doesn't care.*

The following example shows the worker redirecting a message to open up lines of communication between two persons who had stopped speaking.

I was sitting between Mrs. R. and Mrs. H. who had had an argument last week. Mrs. R. said that Mrs. H. had really hurt her feelings. *I said, "Why don't you tell Mrs. H. about it."*

The next two illustrations show the worker redirecting a message within a group in such a way that the entire group is affected by the behavior. In both instances the worker is conveying the message, that he will not do the group's work, as he redirects their message to him back to them.

R. and M. put their chairs next to mine. S. stood up between M. and me. Someone told S. that if she wanted to sit down, there was room on the other side of the table. S. asked everyone to move around. Nobody moved. R. told me to tell S. to go to the other side so that we could get started. *I told R. that if she wanted S. to go elsewhere she could tell S.* She did. Several other people also told S. that she was holding up the works, and S. reluctantly walked around to the other side of the table.

In one of our group sessions we were discussing an issue current at the school. All the interaction was directed at me even though there were two very strong opposing factions who could have been directing their comments to one another. This session occurred

right after the black students had presented their Black History
Week program. The white students were telling me that they
were upset by the content of the program while the black students
were telling me that the program was not meant to offend white
students. Since all these comments were aimed at me, *I suggested
that the comments be directed toward one another rather toward
me.*

TALKING IN THE IDIOM OF THE OTHER

To talk in the idiom of the other is to respond to the other's
disguised, illusory, or veiled messages using the same context
and symbols, treating these as if they were real rather than
unreal, and as if they were overt rather than covert expressions. By responding in the other person's chosen idiom, the
social worker does not force the other to expose himself until
he is ready, and does not force him to cut off the communication. This behavior is used by the social worker when direct,
open communication is not chosen by the client, who,
nevertheless, shows his desire to engage with the worker, albeit
circuituously. It is a means of keeping the lines of communication open despite the sensitivity of the content.

The assumption underlying the use of this behavior is that
open communication can be threatening, almost devastating,
to some persons and to all persons under certain circumstances. For some, discussing problems or even having problems is a sign of weakness that goes against moral values
learned elsewhere. To discuss "personal" things with a
stranger, the social worker, may seem next to impossible. It is
almost as if the person is demeaned by even admitting that he
is not fully in command of his situation all of the time and
needs outside consultation or help. For others, discussing feelings openly goes against life learnings that are deeply en-
grained. In this respect, the American culture has been particularly harsh on men. Many men have learned not to express
feelings, often not to feel, lest they be unmanly. Formal edu-

cation, which has in varying degrees affected the early lives of all persons, has placed value upon thinking, not feeling. Effective thought processes have been rewarded, but no formal teaching is concerned with the feeling or relationship processes in school. Any learning in these areas has been a trial-and-error affair with no grades or medals awarded for success. Moreover, even relatively open individuals may face certain experiences that seem too unusual, or personal, or "crazy" to share with another. The mores of society have been harsh, determining certain feelings and experiences as private, for only the self to attend, or for only the family. Individuals do not relish talking about the unmarried daughter who got pregnant, the husband who embezzled, the son who spray-painted obscenities on the high school wall, for they should somehow be able to manage such matters alone. Shame and guilt take over, and clients may sometimes venture into such threatening territory by offering their concerns in an analogy or in terms of "I have a friend who . . ."

Under such circumstances the social worker talks in the idiom of the other when the other begins this way. He regards this as an opening rather than a continuing charade and, as quickly as possible, moves the communication to a more direct and open level. To talk in the idiom of the other person requires the social worker to recognize the message as an idiom. This involves an analytic skill of looking and listening for metamessages and decoding them. The following illustration shows the social worker involved in such an analytic process as well as in making an idiomatic response.

In the course of a conversation with a ninth-grade, black, male student, he began to speak in terms of the "private school" he used to attend. I suspected that there was something more to this so I responded, *"Tell me what it was like at the private school."* As we discussed the "private school" it became apparent that the school was a school for emotionally disturbed children. The stu-

dent, after testing my opinion as to persons with a history of in-
carceration and mental troubles, offered on his own that the private
school was actually Eastern State Psychiatric School.

In the next illustration of responding in the idiom of the
other, the social worker uses this behavior to help a student admit the problem being discussed is *his* problem.

A student came to tell me about his friend who was afraid to come
to school tomorrow because some kids had threatened to beat him
up. I continued to listen as he described his friend's predicament
in detail. Then I said, "Your friend's in a tough bind." The student agreed and said that his friend was very scared and knew it
could be worse if he let anyone know he was scared. *I said that
his friend must feel very much alone.* The student sat down, banged
his fist on the table, and said, "Shit! What am I going to do?"

The behaviors described are not proposed as necessarily all-
inclusive behaviors that, if mastered, will equip the social
worker to meet all contingencies. Rather, they are the obvious
ones at this time. Other aspects of interaction are known to
require specific acts on the part of the worker but have not
been sufficiently analyzed. For example, the timing of worker
responses and the anticipation of responses beyond the at-the-
moment necessities distinguish the more expert worker from
the novice. Yet, the specifics of such crucial behavior remain
unnamed and unexplained. Furthermore, all interaction
achieves some characteristic pattern determined by such aspects
as size of the unit, adjustments in the individual's tempos and
turn-taking, length of speeches, speed of reactions, tendency to
interrupt, need to control the communication space, and attitudes toward the others. To tailor one's acts to the requirements of these many interactional forces requires some sophisti-
cation, ease, and comfort with the fluid, yet persisting totality—
the interactional Gestalt. These worker behaviors, relating to
rate, speed, and duration, also await further study.

ENGAGING BARRIERS

There are times when a client's description of the pressures impinging upon him remains elusive despite the worker's efforts to engage feelings and information. There are times when a service contract cannot be established despite apparent clarity with respect to the pressures and the task that derives from them. There are times when work on the task specified in the service contract seems to stop. Such events signal the presence of barriers that must be engaged if productive work is to begin and/or continue.

Barriers differ in nature and present themselves in many forms. A particularly sensitive topic on the goal path, for example, can block the work. Social, economic, or political realities can intervene to distract and immobilize. Likewise, an unstated task can rival the stated task. All of these instances are marked by an absence of productive work; hence the need for skill in engaging barriers.

Skill in engaging barriers refers to the use of four specific behaviors. (1) referring to the contract; (2) pointing out obstacles; [11] (3) challenging taboos; and (4) confronting with contradictory reality.

It should be noted here that engaging barriers, while closely related to managing interaction, differs from it in two significant ways. First, interaction management is process-oriented, while engaging barriers is problem-oriented. That is to say, interaction management is concerned with the process of communication, while engaging barriers is addressed to breakdowns in that process. Efforts to manage interaction temporarily interrupt the flow, while efforts to engage barriers involve entry following interruption of the flow by forces other than the worker. A second difference is that managing interaction is specific to the communication process, while engaging barriers deals with both communication and action. Because barriers can block action and/or interaction, barriers must be engaged in both arenas.

REFERRING TO THE CONTRACT

To refer to the contract is to restate the terms of the working agreement. This behavior should be used if, and only if, observable behavior differs from that specified in the service contract.

When the worker refers to contract he tells the others that there is a difference between what "we" said that "we" were going to do and what "we" seem to be doing. There are times when this act is sufficient to remove a barrier temporarily and permit work on the service contract to resume. Use of this behavior is illustrated in the following example.

After the four chiefs of service and I arrived for the meeting to work out details for shortening the intake procedure, there was a lot of talk about different patients, Dr. B.'s wife, and other extraneous subjects. *I waited about five minutes and then said that we had agreed to meet to work out a plan for shortening the intake procedure, but that we didn't seem to be doing that. I wondered if something was getting in the way, or if we could get on with it as planned.*

POINTING OUT OBSTACLES

To point out obstacles is to note the particular event that has gotten in the way of the work.[12] This behavior is appropriate if, and only if, three conditions obtain: (1) observable behavior differs from that specified in the service contract; (2) the worker has referred to contract; and (3) reference to contract did not result in resumption of the work.

It should be noted here that there is nothing inherently worthwhile in the engagement of barriers. Barriers are engaged for the sole purpose of returning to the work essential to lightening the external pressures impinging on the clients. Hence the least engagement of barriers necessary to permit work on the task to resume is in order. And this is consistent with the principle of least contest discussed in Chapter 4. More specifically, when the absence of productive work on the task signals the presence of a barrier, the worker should refer to contract. If, and only if, a barrier is too immediate, or too potent to be set aside, and referring to contract does not result in resumption of work on the stated task, then the worker should point out obstacles.

In the following example, work stops and the worker refers to contract. When her reference does not result in resumption of the work, she points out an obstacle.

In the middle of an angry exchange between Mr. B. and Mrs. K., Miss H. began talking about a young couple she baby-sits for. Several people looked confused, and the planning work stopped. There were a few unrelated comments made, and this was followed by silence. *I restated the terms of the service contract and asked if we could get back to work.* There were some nods, but the silence continued. After a few moments *I said that the group stopped working after Miss H. made her comment and wondered if we could get at what happened so we could get back to the planning.* Someone said that Miss H.'s comment didn't have anything to do with the discussion. Someone else said that it didn't even have anything to do with Miss H. Mr. E. asked Miss H. why did she say that when she did. She said she didn't know, but added that people shouldn't argue because arguing doesn't get you anywhere.

CHALLENGING TABOOS

To challenge a taboo is to mention the unmentionable. This behavior is a special case of pointing out obstacles; hence its use is limited to situations in which the same three conditions obtain.

Personal and social taboos exist to protect self and/or society from the shame, guilt, and embarrassment that accompany encounters in highly sensitive areas of social and personal concern. When such personal or social taboos prohibit the mention of feelings and behaviors pertinent to the task at hand and/or the situation in which work on the task proceeds, these taboos become obstacles to task accomplishment and must be challenged if work is to continue. By mentioning the unmentionable, the potency of the taboo can often be reduced for a while,[13] permitting work to resume.

In the following example, work on the task is blocked by the presence of a barrier. The worker refers to the contract, but this does not result in resumption of the work. Then the worker challenges a taboo.

In accord with the service contract between Mrs. D. and myself, we were to work on getting her a better job. I checked out the job unit and gave Mrs. D. three leads, all of which she refused. She had no leads at all, she told me. There was a brief silence. I reached in vain for more information about her job interests and concerns, while she said nothing but continued to sit in the office looking at me. At this point it was apparent that something was getting in the way, *so I referred to the contract and asked Mrs. D. if we could get onto the work.* She nodded, but said nothing, and we still got nowhere. Then *I said, "Mrs. D., is it hard to work with me because I'm white?"* She said no, that it made no difference to her, but she stopped staring at me and said the problem with the jobs was that she couldn't do the application forms.

Challenging taboos should not be confused with the interaction management behavior, checking out inferences, although at times the two behaviors look alike. Taboos should be challenged only when the work has stopped and reference to contract does not result in its resumption. Checking out inferences, on the other hand, is an effort to validate meaning. Consider the following example.

Early in our contact, Mrs. O. spoke about how "pleasant" it is in this place, a word which I picked up with a question because of its obvious, sarcastic tone. Mrs. O. responded, "Well, you know all the mess and shit we have around. I thought before we moved that it was going to be a nice place, but you know when you're poor. . . . Maybe you don't know what that means. . . ." *I said, "Are you saying that because I am white?"* She answered, "Yes, but also because you don't look like poor people."

The worker mentioned the word "white" not because there was a taboo that blocked the work. Rather, the worker was responding to a message with a request for confirmation that the meaning received was the meaning intended. That is to say, the worker was checking out an inference, not challenging a taboo.

CONFRONTING WITH CONTRADICTORY REALITY

To confront with contradictory reality is to present information that counters distortions by the other.[14] This behavior is usable when (1) information provided by the other is partial, skewed, or otherwise inaccurate; or when (2) the verbal and nonverbal messages of the other are contradictory.

Because people view the world through the filter of their past experience, their values, beliefs, and current concerns, they do not use all the information about the world of people and events that their senses are able to receive. Moreover, because people anticipate the reactions of others and attempt to project particular images of themselves and their situations at different times, they sometimes present only a selective piece of the already selective information they have received. In addition, felt totality, wishful thinking, fear of exposure, and efforts to induce others to respond in certain preferred ways combine further to distort information presented. Such distortions can block work on the task by preventing discussion of relevant concerns and/or precluding a range of choices that the other could consider in selecting action to decrease the pressures impinging upon him. Hence, the worker confronts the other with contradictory reality.

In the first example, the worker confronts an injured veteran with contradictory reality when he misrepresents the differences between living in the hospital and living in the outside world.

Mr. J. said that one thing that made it better to stay in the hospital than to live outside is that there are social workers in the hospital. *I said that there were social workers outside, too.*

In the second example, the worker confronts a former mental patient with contradictory reality when she represents one causal factor as the only cause.

Miss. P. said she knows she can make it with the pills. "These orange pills have marked the beginning of a new life," she said. *I answered, "The pills may help, but they aren't magic. You had a lot to do with the nice difference you made for yourself, too."*

In the third example, the worker confronts an elderly woman with contradictory reality when she inaccurately represents his power.

Mrs. W., a nursing home resident receiving only five dollars per month spending money, asked me to get her a pension. After discussing the eligibility requirements for pensions, social security, and public assistance and jointly acknowledging that she was ineligible for pension or social security and that public assistance was paying for her room and board at the nursing home and providing the five dollars but will not provide more, Mrs. W. said, "I think you are going to take care of it for me." *I said, "I think the outlook for your getting more money is very bad."*

In the fourth example, the worker confronts with contradictory reality when a man's nonverbal message disclaims the validity of his verbal message.

Mr. S. said that everything was all right, but his facial muscles were tense and his expression was troubled. *I told Mr. S. that by the look on his face, everything was not all right.* Then Mr. S. nodded and said that he was just making it.

Part 3

The Organizational Context and the Social Science Base

Chapter 11

The Metawork and the Organizational Context

If we were to look around us at the social workers we know and make a private list of those whom we regard as especially effective, as movers of others, as imaginative innovators, chances are that those on our list would reveal a particular competence in managing the work to be done. They are most likely able to process quickly the diverse stimuli that demand differential responses, to sort out and cut through a morass of detail, and to set priorities. Issues involved in viewing one's work and allocating time differentially, which are matters of skill in priority setting, are major determinants of who will be effective and who will simply be actors in other people's scripts.

This component of priority setting and managing the work exists within every social worker's job. He has some measure of control of how he spends his energies and how he organizes his work. And yet, precious little attention is given to helping students learn to do this. In fact, such know-how is mainly picked up through trial and error if at all. Often how one organizes his work is left to chance, or determined by his personal preferences or comfort with parts of the work rather than by the imperatives of the tasks of service delivery or client need.

As we look back upon the past a serious charge can be raised. Social workers have been busy people, but have they consistently exposed their work to such questions as: "Is all this really necessary?" "Are all of these many activities equally important?" We think not. Therefore, habit, faith, and dogma have ordered the thinking about the "good" service, the "proper" intake procedure, and the necessary recording, more than a continuous critique of the actual merit of these tasks.

THE WORK AND THE METAWORK

Considering all the many activities that bid for worker time and energy, it seems important to separate the work of the service deliverer from what we term the "metawork." The metawork concept will distinguish certain activities, those that facilitate the actual work, from the work itself. In this sense metawork is work about the work. In Chapters 2, 3, and 4 we described many varied activities which are concerned with the client in need and are pursued as the worker's response to the client according to the service contract they work out together. These activities may be with clients, with others in behalf of clients, and with clients in behalf of themselves and others (Quadrant A, D, or B activities). From the service deliverer's perspective, all activities to meet the demands of the client task can be thought of as his service delivery work.

When the rationale for being involved in a particular activity is that it is a response to the client's understanding of what is happening in his behalf, then this is the work of service delivery, whether it occurs with the client himself, whether in person or by telephone, or whether it happens in person or by telephone with others than the client. All other work that may be once removed from direct engagement with the client task is the metawork—the activities that may enhance the work but are aside from the work itself.

Adopting this perspective, such activities as recording, attending staff meetings, participating in interdisciplinary team meetings or case conferences, attending conferences or institutes or workshops, are either agency work or professional development work. Participating in supervision as supervisor or worker, receiving or offering training or staff development is metawork. In this category also must be placed all the red tape, the elaborate accounting, and the formal, written communication system that have grown out of the organization's need to be accountable for the work. Once a distinction is drawn between work with clients and all the supportive work directed to facilitating this work, it may be easier to look at this huge superstructure of metawork to determine its actual versus its illusory enhancement of the basic work. The plight of workers in bureaucratized systems who cannot find time to serve the enormous number of clients at least partially springs from the disproportionate amount of metawork to work, ritualized by the agency through history and tradition.

If we consider all the in-person conferences and meetings, plus all the paper communication as time spent in the name of service *to* clients but not *with* clients, then certain questions must be posed: What proportion of human energy and time within the total operation is directly concerned with clients as opposed to that spent with others in behalf of his needs? What proportion of the energy and time is consumed by the accountability systems? Following these questions, we must consider whether things should be this way.

A benchmark study of these issues [1] was conducted by the Family Service of Philadelphia during 1951–52. This was the first major systematic study of its kind that applied to social services cost accounting principles drawn from the world of commerce and business management. The total staff (administrative, supervisory, casework, and clerical) recorded use of time to the nearest five-minute interval in terms of its ultimate purpose over 252 randomly selected working days not known in advance by the individuals. Eight cost centers were derived from about two hundred activities that staff might perform. Four were considered the basic activities or "production costs" (casework services, group education, professional education or student training, and community activities and planning). The remaining four were viewed as collateral or "share-of-service costs"; that is, those efforts aimed at maintaining the proper quantity and quality level in the basic activities, specifically staff education and development, research, public relations, and general administration.

Further, each of the eight cost centers had a detailed breakdown of activities comprising the category. For example, casework specified subcategories as follows: in-person interviews in the office and outside the office; telephone interviews; collateral in-person interviews in the office and outside the office; collateral telephone interviews; supervision; case consultations; case conferences; case recording; and case assignment routines.

As table 2 shows, $63.66 of each $100 agency expenditure (or 65 percent of all staff time) went to the four basic activities, (production costs), while $36.34 (35 percent) went to the collateral activities, (share of service costs). Within the 65 percent devoted to the basics (casework, group education, professional education, community activities and planning), casework accounted for 56 percent while the other three basic services received 2.9 percent, 2.1 percent, and 3.3 percent respectively. Eighty-six percent of the time spent on the basic activities went to casework, a finding "gratifying" to the executive. A further breakdown of casework by organizational role revealed that it consumed approximately 82 percent of the caseworkers' time,

50 percent of the supervisors' time, 39 percent of clerical time, and 4 percent of administrative time. But what proportion of casework's 86 percent was spent with clients? As the table reveals, only about 27 percent of the casework services (the production part of "interviewing costs") was actually devoted to the direct delivery. We shall consider the other 73 percent metawork.

TABLE 2

DISTRIBUTION OF $100 AMONG CASEWORK SERVICES [a]

	Total Cost	Production Cost	Share of Service Cost
Interviewing costs	$ 42.49	$26.80	$15.69
Case recording	32.15	20.27	11.88
Supervisory conferences	13.17	8.30	4.87
Case consultations	5.77	3.64	2.13
Miscellaneous	6.42	4.29	2.13
Total	$100.00	$63.30	$36.70

[a] Hill and Ormsby

Discussing these findings, Ormsby called for new administrative standards and norms regarding the ratio of total resources to the basic activities and the collateral activities as well as the proportion of in-person interviews to processing procedures (dictation, evaluation, conferencing, consultation, preparation for specific activities) to get away from programs "built up piecemeal and without design other than traditional patterns." [2] Following this elaborate time study, agency attention was aimed at diverting more resources to client interviewing and less to meetings, supervisory conferences, and detail work required in compiling "much seldom-used data." [3] With the impact of seeing that recording and supervisory costs combined exceeded interviewing costs, case summaries were reduced from the usual six or eight pages to two, and oral presentations during supervisory conferences, rather than the

time-hallowed practice of no-transcribed-recording-no-confer-
ence, were initiated. Encouraging as these efforts seem to be,
Ormsby also comments:

It is obviously impossible to expect a caseworker to have, on the
average, more than three client and collateral in-person interviews
per working day, plus necessary telephone interviews, *unless ways
can be found to reduce drastically demands on the worker to record, carry out community and public relations assignments, attend
staff meetings, and so forth.*[4]

Now, some twenty years later, social agencies have not found
the means to reduce the demands on the worker as suggested by
Ormsby. In fact, we are hard put to find more than a handful of
agency-initiated time-cost studies in the literature. Family
Service Association of America (FSAA) encouraged other
member agencies to apply time-analysis studies to measure
agency operations quantitatively [5] and in 1971 reported to its
membership a summary of studies conducted by fifty agencies.[6]
Although analysis of these data from agencies of various sizes
and program emphases did not account for the differences in
time expenditures by either agency size or program, the
amount of staff time devoted to program-related activities was
found to be 86 percent, just as in the Hill-Ormsby study. Of
this amount 39 percent was spent directly with or on behalf of
clients, three quarters of which, or 29 percent, was in interviews
with families (a median amount 2 percent higher than in the
original study). Recording averaged 14 percent, supervision 11
percent, and such metawork as preparation, staff development,
and other activities 21 percent.
    Despite frequent blasts in the news media that aim to expose
mismanagement and waste, there has been little discussion of
similar attempts by agencies to tackle the metawork issue. The
situation today remains much as it was before the Hill-
Ormsby study, except that agency executives cannot feel quite

so comfortable with 86 percent of basic activity devoted to casework and 3.3 percent for community activities (*sic!*) and planning.

In 1972, with fewer systematic controls than the FSAA study, a study of the time allocation of six direct service workers was undertaken in a children's agency. Here it was found that 19 percent was devoted to interviews with clients while 81 percent went to activities needed to support this work (dictation, phone calls, record reading, interview preparation, conferences, meetings, court hearings, and travel). Further, it was found that diagnostic evaluations consumed a minimum of eleven and a half to thirteen hours per child and might take twenty-one and a half hours; maternity intakes could range from three hours and ten minutes to five and a half hours; and foster home applications required from two hours and fifty minutes to three and a quarter hours. We must remember that only one fifth of all these hours was spent with the clients.[7] Briar and Miller discuss this aspect of metawork:

Clients generally do not come to caseworkers simply to be diagnosed —they want and legitimately expect to be helped. . . . Diagnostic efforts are justifiable only insofar as they contribute to the effectiveness of the intervention. . . . If the practitioner has only one treatment approach in his repertoire, then diagnosis is not only unnecessary but meaningless. . . . In many social agencies, it is not uncommon for staff conferences convened to discuss cases to devote fifty-eight minutes to "diagnosis" and two minutes to intervention planning, with little apparent connection between the two discussions.[8]

RECORDING

Another aspect of metawork, often lamented but rarely questioned, is recording. This timeworn standard operating procedure is the greatest consumer of worker time and must either merit the huge investment placed there or be altered. Despite the difficulty of obtaining information on the ratio of clerical time to professional time necessary for completed dictation and the obvious differences among agencies due to matters of size, auspices, and objectives,[9] one estimate drawn from a large, public system indicates that each minute of worker dictation demands from 3.38 to 5.52 minutes of clerical time for its transcription.[10]

Perhaps the time investment, inclusive of dictating, transcribing, and reviewing (reading and discussing by the writer and his superiors), would be justifiable if we were convinced that such procedures made for a better service. But this issue has not been studied. The efficacy of the case record might be reviewed along with a comparison group for whom sketchy, factual notations were all that was recorded to determine the differences in regard to quality, comprehensiveness of service, and client opinion of the service. In such a study, follow-up interviews with former clients to assess their retrospective view of the service as well as their current life situation would be a primary source of data to support or invalidate our faith in the case record. Only then would we approach some evaluation of the qualitative difference in services rendered as a function of the kind of recording that accompanied the service.

It is likely that valuation of the case record stems more from the time-honored system of supervision than from the demands of service. That is to say, the case record is the major instrument for learning not only about the client, but about the worker's skills, and in terms of this latter function, it serves as the primary means for on-the-job teaching/learning. When most supervisors and administrators received their professional education, the process record was at the core of their learning. Hence, supervisors tend to be familiar with and to prefer this medium, and may find it difficult to consider any other system of looking at one's work as equally "professional." Perhaps the case record would have assumed a less central position in the

supervisory process had the professional education of supervisors and administrators devoted comparable time to such
methods for helping others as examination of group processes
and dynamics, and their operation and application in diverse
contexts: collegial self-help groups, case conferences, and
staff training. But the essence of teaching helping skills was
viewed as inhering in the detailed case record. Moreover, an
equally discriminating way to record the service other than
by detailed descriptive accounts has not yet been devised; nor
have various media other than the individual supervisory
conference been utilized to any great extent.

This state of affairs exists not because the individual case
record and the individual supervisory contact where it is
processed and reviewed are the only possible approaches, nor
necessarily the best approaches. Rather, these methods are
what most workers know how to use. But, despite familiarity
with the *status quo* and the very real lack of elaborate alternative mechanisms for supervision, too much time which should
be spent delivering services is consumed with recording and
reviewing records that frequently aim to demonstrate (to his
supervisor) the worker's perceptiveness. As Briar and Miller
indicate: "Caseworkers are not paid to write biographies or to
seek out arcane subtleties of the client's experiences unless they
can demonstrate that these activities increase their effectiveness
in helping clients." [11]

The worker's detailed record of the client's response to his
effort to help often contains as much biased, prejudicial, and
possibly perjorative information as it does facts. And while the
facts and bare history provide continuity when workers leave,
agencies might have fewer "hopeless" clients if workers were
freed from the biased accounts of their predecessors and could
form their own impressions from the freshness of the new
contact.

The case record that aims to demonstrate the worker's sensitivity to diagnostic cues is focused upon the client and his problem. These accounts mainly reveal the client's reactions and feelings plus the worker's judgments of their meaning. They do not equally record the worker's reactions and feelings as one major element that affects everything the client does; usually, the worker's part of the transaction is taken as a given. For example, workers do not record moments when they felt intimidated or bored or uncertain, nor do they admit in the written review that the anger noted on the part of the client might have been aroused by their ineptitude. Supervisors review these accounts and use them to help the worker see his blind spots, biases, or other insensitive behavior by making their own inferences from what *was* and what *was not* recorded. This process often becomes the game of "I see something you don't see," an important mechanism for assuring some supervisors that they really know more than the workers and hold a vital place in the agency hierarchy.[12]

Another question must be raised about the case record that focuses on a description of client behavior. Does the client know, as part of the service contract initially worked out with him, that a written record of his case will be kept which will reside in the agency file for all time? Does he know the kind of information that will be in his record? Does he know that his attitudes, feelings, and so forth will be recorded there, possibly subject to court order if evidence about him is desired at some future time, possibly open to public scrutiny? Social work as a profession has not yet achieved community sanction for privileged communication, as have psychiatry, law, and the ministry, and cannot completely assure confidentiality to the client. Surely, we believe, the client's understanding of this situation and his agreement to such documents are a *sine qua non* for work in his behalf. And written documents should be kept with the hazards of public viewing in mind.

Lengthy, descriptive, inadvertently biased documents, whose

existence the client may be unaware of, load the files of social agencies. The reading and processing time devoted to their use with each social worker seems to account for a major investment of supervisory energies. From the perspective of service demands and the validity of the process record, their value is questionable. But to question the validity of the record brings the pervasive pattern of one-to-one supervision into question as well. For the record is demanded and justified by the supervision. That is to say, the questionable process record is the instrument by which the supervisor can know what each worker is doing with the clients, since the actual transaction is conducted in privacy. The record is the tool for the supervisor and is used for teaching service deliverers. This leads to the question: How long does it take for the worker to be viewed as an autonomous professional responsible for the quality of his own work?

TRADITIONAL SUPERVISION

The service deliverer cannot accord self-determination to clients when he suffers from a gross lack of professional self-determination within the bureaucratic hierarchy. Unlike the client, the worker cannot stop going to conferences when he believes that they are not helpful to him. Nor does he possess action groups to advocate for his professional entitlement against the power structure of his agency. The influence of supervisor upon worker is potent and flows from several bases of power: legitimate (the agency sanctions this role); expert (though sometimes questioned, the supervisor knows more); informational (the supervisor has particular information to which the worker does not have access); reward and coercive (the promotion, increment, and, with respect to this, the image of the worker rests in the supervisor's hands).[13]

Goffman views the social behavior of persons as careful performances that create a "front" or an impression. Individuals

define the situations they encounter in such a way that they
guide and control the impressions that others obtain of them;
by using various techniques, they aim to present a favorable
self-image.[14] With respect to his supervisor, the social worker
expends considerable energy on his own "impression management" out of self-interest from his low power status. His differences with the supervisor might be labeled overreactive or
unconscious resistance.[15] To approach the problems that stem
from such normative judgments by supervisors, agencies must
begin somehow to convey the message to the workers that they
have the skills necessary to accomplish their work, and set
about deploying the energies of the higher echelon staff to
devise ways for systematically stretching horizons and stimulating all the service staff to exploration of the practice.

The complexity of the supervisory role in social work, a role
that combines administrative and educational functions in one
person, has been discussed in the literature,[16] especially since
Austin highlighted the dilemma and urged that these two
functions be separated.[17] But as Hanlan points out, there have
been no formal, permanent, structural revisions within agencies
to support attempts to redefine the supervisor's role.[18] The
present pattern not only is time-consuming and inhibiting to
the avowed professional norm of individual autonomy, but
authoritarian in consequences. The almost exclusive reliance
upon the mechanism of close one-to-one supervision as the
major means for keeping agency practice in tune with service
requirements is increasingly questioned in the literature in
regard to its influence upon conformity more than innovation,
its power over the professional destinies of the staff, and its
antiegalitarian emphasis.[19]

The Purposes of Recording. Written records serve three
purposes: (1) surveillance, (2) continuity, and (3) on-the-job
training. These purposes should be clearly separated from each
other to insure the integrity and utility of each. The surveil-

lance aspect is statistical and has to do with numbers of contacts, numbers of inquiries, kinds of problems, hours spent,
monies spent, and so forth. Continuity is provided by a record
of service, which should also be factual and summarized. Each
agency has certain purposes for which these records of service
are used, and these should be known by the social service
deliverer before he produces written records. Probably the
purpose (and thus the format) will differ according to who
uses the records and to what ends. For instance, when social
workers are in interdisciplinary settings and their notations are
placed centrally along those of doctors, attendants, or other
staff, the nature of the information will differ from the recording made within a social service department or a social agency.

Generally, records are a collection of information that is
needed to document or convey detail to another source concerned with the agency's program and services. The kind of
information detailed in case records, forms, and all written
accounting should always be viewed from the perspective of
what its use will be. For example, the elaborateness of social
histories containing voluminous questions on the client's background should be reviewed from the perspective of how all
this information will help in offering services, and each non-
essential question should be viewed with alarm.

Agencies do not look to new workers to attack the record-
keeping system as a first order of involvement. However, as
the service deliverer becomes familiar with his setting, it is not
beyond the realm of possibility that some of his energies will
be directed at this aspect of the work as one way to push the
agency to engage in continuous self-appraisal.

As a general heuristic, the service deliverer's focus in his
record of service should be upon *his* activities with the client.
For example, his written account might include date of contact, tasks performed, telephone calls and contacts made with
various sources in behalf of the client, outcomes of these con-

tacts, and next appointment or other steps arranged. Furthermore, the recording should *not* be about the client's behavior or responses to the worker.

This type of service record would provide continuity, enable new workers to pick up with clients and know what had happened in the past, and avoid many of the problems of biases, value judgments, and misuse. Clearly, this approach to recording with its emphasis upon the specific things done with or on behalf of the client rather than upon detailing client responses to worker statements or the worker/client relationship dynamics is a key element of a structural approach to practice. The emphasis here is upon the task to be accomplished and the steps taken toward the goal.

Other kinds of written records might be undertaken for the avowed purpose of worker on-the-job training. Such records might form the basis for teaching and staff development in individual or group supervisory conferences, team meetings, training sessions, and so forth. For these purposes as much detail as possible is desirable, especially in those portions of a contact with a client that the worker himself sees as problematic and with which he wishes help. The detailed written account of the worker and client in action, screened through the grid of the worker's judgment of the essential elements after the event, can be a vital teaching/learning instrument. It is, of course, screened, being the worker's version of what happened; limited by what he noticed and remembered, his willingness and facility in using words to describe the total interaction, and the capability of words for expressing experience.

A detailed record might be composed of two parts, narrative and analysis. In the narrative portion the minutiae of the interaction are detailed in process, in "he said–I said" fashion. The worker's preparation for reviewing his work should include underlining, and noting in the margin what skills he used, what principles he was following, and so forth. In the analysis portion, the worker would discuss why he did what he did, what underlying theory or theories he was operating from, and what questions he has.

Another form of on-the-job records for worker development are the notes kept by the worker for his own use, perhaps as reminders of themes to pursue, issues to raise in the future, shifts in the patterns of interaction. As workers form the habit of keeping their own logs aimed toward particulars upon which they wish to focus their energies and attention, they will come to feel a special kind of responsibility for their own progress on the job.

Another approach that might stimulate worker learning and improved performance is the use of one-way screens where others can view and evaluate the work. For on-the-spot feedback and suggestions, a telephone can connect the worker and the viewer behind the one-way screen so that suggestions or cautions, for example, can be telephoned in while the interaction is in progress. Clearly, the only way to obtain a complete account of an interaction is through videotaping so all that is said or not said can be captured. And even this mechanism is limited by the focus of the camera at any particular moment; hence its account is not fully complete. Audiotapes can provide documentation of the verbal part of the transaction, possibly useful for later study and review.

It may seem that electronic equipment is too expensive for agencies to mount. But if we can imagine that new modalities and formats for on-the-job training will replace older patterns and forms, considerable monies are going into supervisory salaries that reorganization efforts might tap. A primary implicaion, not fully elaborated here, is that a new culture surrounding agency work must be established, including new norms for transforming into a public matter open for group attention and peer directed learning the privateness and loneliness of a practice shared only with the supervisor.

We have reviewed recording, used for purposes of surveillance, continuity, and on-the-job training, because of a concern that the time invested in writing and processing records through conferences with supervisors exceeds that spent directly with clients. We have suggested the need for differentiation among the purposes of records and proposed some new formats which might be utilized to distinguish the record of service that is kept assumedly in the client's (and agency's) behalf from the documents whose primary *raison d'être* is for teaching the workers. Naturally, any restructuring of the record-keeping system calls into question the system of supervision that such recording supports.

We have alluded to the need for change in the traditional supervisory arrangements of agencies, a conclusion also reported by Schwartz and Sample as one that does not contribute to the most effective performance of service deliverers.[20] It seems imperative that agencies must critically review present hierarchical supervisory arrangements and restructure roles so that becoming a supervisor is not the only route upward in the system.

If the educational function were separated from the administrative function of supervision, then major energies could be devoted to attending to quality control, through clearly administrative supervisors and to the introduction of new technologies and patterns of services geared to meet the service goals through training programs specially devised to meet staff needs for learning and innovation on the job.

The role of trainer seems especially important as an alternative to the emphasis on supervision. Recent manpower studies suggest the efficacy of team approaches that include members of diverse professional and educational backgrounds for delivering better services than have certain approaches in the past.[21] Trainers should be specialists in using group approaches with staff and able to teach staff to work in teams. Implied here is a group-based training approach within agencies. At the staff level the substitution of the small-team group for idea exchange and decision-making may, as has been demonstrated in other organizations,[22] provide a direction for creating new norms within the service delivery systems that stress peer judgment and mutual responsibility in practice.

A RATIONALE FOR ATTENTION TO METAWORK

In considering the issue of work and metawork we have inevitably been drawn into areas previously excluded from the core curriculum of the student in direct service methodologies. Such areas as organizational theory, power and decision-making within and outside the social agency, superior/subordinate role relationships and their variable patterns have been largely reserved for those choosing to specialize in administration, supervision, and planning service delivery. Preparation of the direct service pratictioner concentrated on the complexities of the worker-client relationship.

Our central thesis is that service deliverers must know as much about their interrelatedness to others within the system, to the ways organizations move and shift or stick and stay, as they need to know about their own roles with clients. For in large part their work with clients is as much affected by the forces of the organization within which they operate as by their own efforts with a given client. So long as the organizational arrangements are viewed as givens and the service deliverer directs his professional understanding only toward the client, so long will the social agencies continue to operate with the bureaucratic hierarchical structure predominant—the present-day picture—and so long will the side effects of this structure (low morale, frustration, conformity, and undistinguished individual performance) persist.

In a sense, the service deliverer must have double vision: partly he must focus on those coming for service, partly on the arrangements within which he must work, so that his energies directed to the latter help the agency remain accountable and responsive to client need. For just as the client is central in defining the pressures he faces, so is the worker the one who knows best how his agency environment supports or hinders his work. He must bring to bear as much knowledge, understanding, and skillful handling of self and others within the organization as he knows he must bring to the worker-client relationship. Rather than being guided only by emotion, opinion, or belief, the service deliverer needs to use planful and purposeful behavior in his role within the system to help the organization renew itself from the inside. He is an interested party who can contribute to the evolution of new structures, patterns, and processes if he understands and takes this part of his professional assignment seriously.

Thus, while our primary concern is with the actual delivery of the service, we intend to emphasize by some, albeit cursory, attention to the organizational arrangements in which the service is offered that the service deliverer's knowledge and legitimate deployment of time and energy to conceptualizing this aspect of the work affects his effectiveness in the delivery of services. More complete discussion of organizations as context and the implication of these forces upon social services can be found in the literature.[23]

THE ORGANIZATION

When a problem is sufficiently widespread that it threatens the general welfare of the community, it is recognized as a social problem, and at least part of it is marked for public action. That action may be aimed at alleviating or managing the problem, or diminishing the potency of its deleterious effects. Because public action requires resources that may have been or potentially will be committed to other aspects of community life, because different vested interest groups in the community designate different aspects of community life as priorities in the allocation of resources, and because what is problematic for some segments of the community is advantageous to other segments of the community, there is conflict over both goals and means. These conflicts are resolved through a process of trade-offs among the competing groups; hence, the social task that emerges and the amount and type of resources committed for its accomplishment represent a compromise,[24] as opposed to a determination reached by parties exclusively concerned with resolution of the problem. The compromise-task is then assigned to an agency charged with accomplishing it with the limited resources allocated. It should be noted that this political compromise is frequently responsible for the off-target activity of many social agencies which bear the brunt of public criticism for not accomplishing what they were never mandated to accomplish.

Within the restrictions of the political definition of the task to be accomplished and the amount and kind of resources allocated for this purpose, the agency which is established must organize itself to deliver and account for services delivered. To a great extent, the point of organization is to limit the number of behavioral alternatives available to individual members of the system so that performance is more predictable. To this end, roles with expectations supported by a system of rewards and punishments are elaborated, and rules for the interaction of role incumbents are set down. These rules specify both particular actions to be performed and the conditions under which their performance is to occur and are codified in a formal set of policies and procedures. In general, role differentiation in a social agency is based on the unequal distribution of power rather than on functional specialization, although the latter is not entirely absent. That is to say, less powerful role incumbents report to, and are directed by, more powerful role incumbents, such as supervisors, who, in turn, report to, and are directed by, incumbents of roles at still higher levels in the hierarchy. In contrast to this is the corporation with specialized units for promotion, design, research and development, training, and so on.

FORCES CONFOUNDING AGENCY OPERATIONS

It is perhaps the most theoretically interesting and pragmatically demoralizing organizational phenomenon that maintenance of the roles and rules initially devised to facilitate accomplishment of the service goal ultimately becomes a goal of equal if not greater importance than that service goal. That is to say, means become ends in themselves, frequently obscuring, if not usurping, the primacy of the original mission. And beyond the formal role relationships based on power differentials, an informal organization based on interpersonal attraction develops, the maintenance of which diverts still more energy from accomplishment of the service goal. To the external impediments to the service delivery posed by political decisions regarding definition of the social task and allocation of resources are added the internal obstructions posed by institutionalized efforts to maintain the established patterns of formal and informal role relationships.

Further confounding service delivery is competition between vested interest groups at the social agency level. Professionals from different disciplines with diverse primary orientations, bureaucratic functionaries, clients, and those who say they speak for clients all have special subgoals for which they seek organization acceptance in the form of resource allocation. In view of this, Heraud suggests that organization theory predicated on such assumptions as common goals, shared values, and unity of purpose (an integration model) is not useful for understanding social agencies and should be replaced by a theory which presupposes no central value system, multiple, vague goals, and goal conflict that arises from forces outside the organization as much as within it (conflict model).[25] Adding to goal conflict as well as means conflict in the social agency setting is the current issue regarding the viability of method-based orientations for the delivery of social work services. And a challenge to method is a challenge to the historical justification of professional social work activity and the huge body of policies and procedures, agency rules, and professional norms that evolved to support such practice—the fabric of agency life.

Thus, it is one thing to distinguish work from metawork, and another to recognize the unresolved issues surrounding both concepts deriving from disagreement over goals and means. Further, with so much power and vested interest deployed to the metawork, including statuses and identities tied to the current role expectancies, the problems inhering in restructuring roles are complex. For roles are filled by people, and new role expectancies demand different skills.

Still another conflict characteristic of social agencies is that between professional autonomy and administrative control. Much as in the fields of health, education, and business, the strain within the social service system is between those forces supporting standard agency policy and practice and the new, the "heretical," the different way of thinking and acting. On one side is the administrator's push for quality control, for assurance that all clients can expect to receive a somewhat similar kind of attention and response at a given agency, no matter who their social worker is, while on the other side is the push for autonomy from the individual social workers.

All too often, much as the idealistic young schoolteacher gradually sinks into the morass of the public education system as he is systematically shown by his system's rewards and sanctions that his beliefs and goals are naïve and misguided, so is the newly arrived social worker often gradually ground down to fit the *status quo* under the guise of being taught by his more experienced peers and supervisors the realities of life. The service deliverer, bent on his own image management, finds chances for advancement greater if he meets the expectations of those who evaluate his work. He prefers being liked to being disliked, and may not have the energy and confidence to follow his own internal gyroscope and make waves within the organization. Thus, it is not surprising that many prefer to accommodate themselves to the agency rather than engage in the struggle needed to change it. The trade-off is autonomy and diversity in the interest of uniformity, clarity, and accountability.

Bennis suggests that most organizational theorists have concentrated upon the internal structure and dynamics of systems rather than on their relationship to the external environment and their capacity to adapt to and shape it.[26] Using the concepts of reciprocity and adaptability, those dealing with internal forces and those dealing with the organization environment, Bennis thinks the future strains for bureaucracies reside in the organization's lack of flexibility and adaptability to its externalities. In his view the future demands organizations that are highly adaptive, rapidly changing, temporary systems, attuned to the rapidly changing environment. They should be organized around problems to be solved by people differentiated not according to rank or role, but according to skill and training. These differentiated units should be coordinated by "linking-pin" personnel able to mediate between the various project groups.[27]

A REVIEW OF THE METAWORK

If one adopts a structural perspective not only toward the client and his predicament but toward the organization offering the services, then it follows that agency effectiveness, staff morale productivity, and possibilities for program development stem, for better or for worse, from the forces impinging upon the worker. They are not created by him. The intricate network of patterned transactions between client, worker, and service delivery system are one focus for attention. Another is the linkage of the organization and its exchange processes with other diverse social institutions and organizations, its external environment.

The focus for development cannot be exclusively upon the staff, no matter how well-intended and enlightened the administrator's view; rather it is the organization that must continuously be developing. In one sense, focus upon staff development, which may appear progressive on the surface, is a gross example of institutionalized victim blaming; as if the organization's problems would be solved if only staff were better prepared to do their jobs. To presume that the problems are a function of individual attributes or interpersonal interactions is to approach a complex of forces at the wrong level of analysis.[28] For systems have properties independent of the individual actors; roles and norms may be begun by people, but once established they exist independently of them and exert a powerful force on the people. No matter how caring an individual may be when he comes to work at the Department of Public Assistance, once he is involved in its workings, the rules force him to be otherwise. If the locus of the organization's problems is considered to reside in the staff, then the spotlight is there rather than on the total organization and all the complexities of the internal and external networks that make the organization function.

No amount of staff development can singlehandedly deal with structural problems. Lectures on racism aimed to change staff attitudes will not affect the work if policies and procedures are racist. Nor will community mental health centers work toward their mandated goals of prevention and serve people in the community so long as the center is paid on a per capita basis for only those who walk into the building for treatment. Nor will children's agencies ever devote much real energy to maintaining children in their own homes, and deliver the material and other resources needed to support this program, so long as child welfare agencies are reimbursed per capita for numbers in foster care or group homes. Nor will medical social workers be able to deal with the gross social problems of massive segments of the population that accompany illness, so long as hospital policy directs major resources to the crises surrounding in-hospital treatment, so long as the doctors decide which patients need the social services.

The profound effects of the external forces, those vagaries of the political climate which become translated into uncertain resources that are always up for question, can make quixotic affairs of even the best conceived plans of social workers. The compromise between what is desirable and what is feasible can make any discussion seem fantastic. Withal, these issues are discussed as if it were possible to follow the desirable. The presumption then, is that social work as a profession will clarify its priorities. Following this, it will need to have a voice in defining its role rather than having this decided by others.

Assuming, then, that social work sees and wants to deliver more than the coping and rehabilitative functions, wants involvement also in preventive and developmental social welfare concerns, and assuming that greater clarity about levels of tasks and skills is being taught to larger segments of the population concerned with human services, then in order to implement new directions those in the social agencies must be ready to bear the anguish of restructuring the delivery system's potential to deliver. Internal reorganization will be unpleasant for those who bear the strain of the shifts. And the internal stresses and strains will obviously be exacerbated by the uncertainties and insecurities that derive from external threats. Likewise, service will suffer while organizations are changing, for there will be less energy for production of services. Maslow questions Theory Y management principles [29] on similar grounds:

You cannot trust people with a key to the pantry when most people are starving or when there is not enough food to go around. . . . if there were one hundred people and there was food for ten, and ninety of these hundred had to die, then I would make sure that I would not be one of those ninety and I'm quite sure that my morals and ethics and so on would change very radically to fit the jungle situation.[30]

The point here is that just as humane attitudes—everyone can be trusted, has the impulse to achieve, does not need the security of role to justify dominance—are dependent upon certain other circumstances, so social agencies can be innovative only when we assume they have succeeded at Maslow's "safety-need" level.[31]

But social agencies stand midway between a watchful, critical public that begrudges and finances reluctantly the basic social requirements of the poor and of the suffering who are hidden from public view as much as possible as well as of those in need whose alienation, anger, and despair increase daily with their "social" services and the conditions surrounding their delivery. All too often staff energy is diverted from service provision by the breathless rush to keep up with the needs of the clients, with the changes in requirements and policy regulations, and with the gaps created by the shifting personnel who move through the bureaucracies and on to less troublesome work places. One recent comprehensive study of a public assistance agency reported the probabilities of new direct service staff staying even one year on the job as only 45 percent.[32]

Thus dependent upon the vagaries of public opinion and legislative enactment of resources, the social welfare organization can hardly be counted upon to provide services from a context of stability. Both the service and the spirit of the staff that delivers them are subject to the inconsistent, piecemeal, and shifting resources accorded from year to year by the influentials in the economic/political realm. Social agencies have not "made it" at Maslow's basic safety-need level, and the ethics that order interorganizational life can hardly be humane and benevolent. Rather, interorganizational life is perilous and mirrors the insecurities and uncertainties of the day-to-day lives of the clients.

It is beyond the scope of this book to dwell at length on the organizational arrangements. Our major aim is to suggest that the future of the welfare system demands organizations that dispense social services possess stability, an aura of legitimacy, and value to the larger society (as has the armed forces system) so that the administrators can concentrate upon deploying necessary talent and resources to making the work place an exciting environment—one with career opportunities and personal enrichment for those who work there. When this happens, it will be possible to devote monies to research and development (a necessary, valued component in commercial enterprises), to refinement and improvement of social welfare's products (services), and to allocation of resources proportionate to the need of any organization for upgrading and attending to the quality of staff performance. Such an orientation to services will depend upon structural arrangements that undergird the value of continuing staff development and training and new linkages with the universities and institutions that can provide specialized educational opportunities for theoretical and methodological study and advancement.

CONCLUSION

Proceeding from the assumption that organizational arrangements affect the quality of services as much as, if not more than, an individual practitioner's skill, we have described some of the internal and external forces that impinge upon the social agency and its central resource—its staff. Priority setting as a skill distinguishes the social worker who is in control of his work load from the one whose work load is in control of him. And we have found that strategic deployment of energies at the organizational level can be learned at the same time as one learns how to be and act with clients. We believe this element has been neglected in the education of students in favor of concentration upon learning methods of practice. One consequence of such an intensive focus upon the worker-client relationship and the exclusion of comparable attention, such as focus upon theoretical and practical knowledge about organizational dynamics, has been a view of the agency as a given—perhaps a necessary evil with which the worker must identify, or subvert covertly, or ignore as much as possible ("I will be different from the other workers you knew"). Surely, the consequence has not been a practitioner who sees the organization as potentially fluid and capable of shifts and alternative patterns in its structural organization, not merely in its potential for adding on new practice inventions.

Because of our conviction that the circumstances of service provision can make *the* difference provided the agency has a resource to provide that is of consequence to clients, we have described some of the organizational arrangements that we believe are variables, that are subject to change provided the service deliverer sees them as changeable and devotes energy to devising means for affecting organizational arrangements. Central to employing change efforts toward the organization in which one works is knowledge about the intricacies of the problems and belief in the possibility of organizational change. A structural approach to practice demands that its basic stance, one of adjusting the environment to the person rather than the person to the environment, also applies to the agency as environment for the worker. This is a difficult, not an impossible, assignment.

We have focused upon certain key elements that are potentially changeable, not once-for-all-time givens. In this category are the time-worn, cumbersome recording practices of agencies and the hierarchially based system of close one-to-one supervision that was congenial to a practice theory that emphasized an individualistic orientation to the client who would grow and change through a relationship. We suggest that practitioners cannot at one and the same time accord the client a central position in determining the tasks they will work on together and experience less than this consideration himself from his superiors in the organization. It seems to have been far easier for the higher-ups to embrace a consumer-oriented partnership with those who come for services than to apply a similar orientation to staff decision-making and planning around service emphases, priorities, policies, procedures, and so forth. For there is support for consumer power in present-day ideology and in the literature of social work and other professions. But, on the other hand, there seems to be little support within institutionalized professions such as social work, where the professionals work together under the sponsorship of an organization, for a worker-oriented partnership with the administration.

Beyond dogma of the past and habit are possibilities for enhancement of the basic work of agencies once all levels in the present hierarchy are scrutinized from the perspective of effective service rather than role-related self-interest. As one means for moving toward such a review, we have proposed the concept of metawork to stand for all the work about the work, and have argued that whether or not this metawork actually enhances the work of the service delivery is open to question. Toward the end of stimulating increased interest in self-evaluation of service (rather than waiting for others to do this to the service systems), we have presented some data derived from time-cost studies, some brief consideration of the red tape that ties up the bureaucracies, and passing attention to the politically determined external influences that may have diverted the administrators of social agencies from deploying primary attention and resources to the quality of work life of the staff. Our aim in highlighting these internal and external complexities which the social welfare organizations will continue to have to contend with is to leave the reader with the challenge that effective services will be offered more readily when the obligation for continuous change rests equally upon the organization and its staff.

Chapter 12

Social Science and Social Work Practice

A theory is a set of concepts and propositions that presents an organized view of phenomena. It tells us which of the many factors in a given social situation are important and it provides categories for classifying, and thereby imparting meaning to what we observe.

The particular meaning which a given theory imparts to a particular set of observed behaviors is not necessarily the only meaning that could be given to them. Other theories may provide different, even antithetical explanations of the same phenomenon. Consider, for example, five different theories of the etiology of social problems.

According to anomie theory, social problems arise when changes in values and goals disrupt the normative order and weaken the authority of social institutions, resulting in social disorganization, or anomie. An alternative theory is the theory of individual deviance, which accounts for social problems in terms of individuals who, by reason of social, intellectual, or emotional deficiency, violate social norms. From yet another perspective, social problems occur when different segments of society hold conflicting values, and what is problematic for one group is advantageous for another group. A fourth approach combines aspects of anomie theory with aspects of conflict theory and suggests that social problems result from a discrepancy between values and actual conditions, between conflicting groups and the way in which resources are distributed. From a fifth perspective, social problems are the product of unintegrated social change. That is, they arise when conflicting behavior patterns exceed the capacity of society's integrating mechanisms.[1]

Each of these theories emphasizes different aspects of a complex social situation and offers a different explanation for the same phenomenon. Thus whatever theory one follows, it directs his attention to certain variables (not necessarily the only variables) and gives a particular meaning (not necessarily the only meaning) to the observed values of these variables. In other words, theory tells us what to observe and what to infer from our observations. Hence, when we accept a particular social theory we are agreeing to see the world of people and events in a particular way, and this agreement has implications for our actions and consequences for the populations we serve. If we accept the theory of individual deviance, for example, we would probably attempt to deal with social problems by directing our actions toward rehabilitating, resocializing, or otherwise changing the behavior of those who violate the norms of society. If we accept conflict theory, or a combination of conflict theory and anomie theory, on the other hand, we might well work toward a redistribution of resources and parity among conflicting segments of society.

Despite Heraud's statement that "there is nothing inherent in the sociological enterprise which leads *to* the practice of social work,"[2] when sociological theory is used to observe and interpret phenomena there is much inherent in the sociological enterprise that leads the practice of social work. Every theory is predicated on the theorist's assumptions about the world of people and events, assumptions which are not part of the theory per se, but are implicit in the selection and corresponding omission of variables, the proposed relationships among variables selected, and the methodology employed in testing the propositions. In Gouldner's terms, these potent yet elusive presuppositions are the theorist's domain assumptions, "often internalized long before the intellectual age of consent." [3] They derive from the theorist's own class and cultural background and reflect his vested interests as a member of society. That is, the theorists' domain assumptions are political in nature, and the theory which they shape has political implications. Thus, the social worker's selection of some theory from among all possible theories is a political decision. Therefore, any effort to articulate the particular aspects of social science knowledge essential to social work practice in general, and the structural approach to social work practice in particular, must begin with recognition of the political nature of social science theory. In other words, social science theory is political both in content and consequence, and the myth of ojectivity must be exploded before we can get down to the business of deciding how to view the phenomenological world.

THE POLITICS OF CONCEPT FORMATION

Since the smallest unit of theory is the concept, it seems reasonable to begin exploring the politics of social science by examining the political content and consequences of concept formation and the conceptualizing process.

A concept is a unit of meaning. It is a cognitive category for organizing discriminably different stimuli that meet certain criteria which demarcate the category into a single group or class. It can be likened to a box with a label on it, a box in which a range of experience can be classified so that a glance

at a particular person or event recalls the pertinent label and
gives meaning to the particular person or event perceived. A
concept is a convenient way to summarize and store an array
of detail. The concept *tree,* for example, subsumes maples,
elms, oaks, firs, palms, and many others. Similarly, the concept
home subsumes house, igloo, and tepee. To conceptualize is to
sort people, things, and events into a set of cognitive categories,
or boxes.

It is important to note that concepts do not exist in the
external world. There is no such thing as a tree that exists
separate and apart from elms, maples, oaks, or some specific
instance of the concept. Nor is there a home without house,
igloo, or tepee. And it is because concepts do not exist in the
external world that concept formation is political in character.
We invent concepts in order to make sense out of the world of
people and events, and, except for concepts provided by the
physical world [4] which are presumably universal, the concepts
we invent are largely determined by the interests and occupa-
tions of our culture and the language reflecting that culture
which we learn to speak as children. According to Bruner,
Goodnow, and Austin:

The categories in terms of which man sorts out and responds to the
world around him reflect deeply the culture into which he is born.
The language, the way of life, the religion and science of a people:
all of these mold the way in which a man experiences the events
out of which his own history is fashioned. In this sense, his personal history comes to reflect the traditions and thought-ways of
his culture, for the events that make it up are filtered through the
categorical systems he has learned.[5]

To the Hanunoo of the Philippines, for example, rice is a
staple food, and differences in types of rice are consequently
of great importance. Therefore, the Hanunoo have names for
ninety-two different types of rice, while we put all ninety-two

into one box labeled "rice." [6] And since the Wintu economy
is based on cattle raising, the Wintu have names for many
different types of cows.[7]

THE THEORIST IN THE THEORY

In 1936, Stevens wrote:

The purpose of science is to invent workable descriptions of the
universe. Workable by whom? By us . . . we formulate descriptions
of the world as we see it and according to our convenience.[8]

The theorist is, first of all, a person. He is influenced by
his own class and cultural background and his own vested
interests as a member of society. And these biases which he
brings to the theory-building enterprise are, in Gouldner's
terms, intellectually consequential, hence theory-shaping.[9] It is
no mere accident, for example, that psychoanalytic theory with
its emphasis on Oedipal conflict was conceived in a Germanic
culture with an authoritarian family tradition. Nor was it by
chance that Talcott Parsons, the product of an optimistic American culture and a man for whom success within the system was
a personal reality,[10] constructed a social theory that presumes
the viability of the *status quo* and classifies social problems
as the result of accidental or temporary breakdowns in the
existing order. For Parsons, the deepest reality of society was
its unity. For Marx, whose cultural and personal realities were
quite different, division and class conflict were the central
realities.

The theorist does not merely respond to a stimulus as if it
were irrelevant to his own concerns. Rather, to use Mead's
formulation, the theorist, like others, has a response inside him,
and he seeks a stimulus to which he can make that response.[11]

In view of this, it is not surprising that Kurt Lewin, a German Jew, chose to compare democratic and autocratic leadership styles and found democratic leadership the superior. Nor is it surprising that, given the prevailing social definition of blacks, investigators from Van Evrie [12] in 1870 to Moynihan [13] and Jensen [14] in the 1960s have "found" blacks inferior to whites. According to Jones:

> . . . what they [social scientists] did was provide scientific explanations to justify the social patterns of belief, for science is not so objective that it remains untouched by the social framework within which it operates, for interpretations of data, and indeed the particular effects one chooses to study are shaped by the prevailing conception of reality that exists for a given society at a given time. . . . whites believed blacks to be inferior . . . white scientists believed them inferior and their findings proved blacks inferior. This proof reinforced the belief . . . to social prejudices had been added "impartial" scientific proofs. . . . Until the beliefs of the society change, the kinds of discoveries made by scientists about blacks will not change. [15]

The relationship of belief to scientific discovery is hardly limited to racial issues, however, for beliefs account, in large part, for a common fallacy of inferring causation from association. Two variables are causally related if, and only if, a change in one variable (the cause) produces a change in the other variable (the effect). Striking a match produces a flame. Two variables are associated, but not causally related, when knowledge of one variable enables prediction of the other variable, but a change in one does not produce a change in the other. To illustrate a noncausal association between two variables, Anderson cites the relationship between the number of mules and the number of Ph.D.s in a state:

> It is a fact that states with the greatest number of mules have the fewest Ph.D.s, and vice versa. Does this fact mean that number of

mules and number of Ph.D.s are causally related? Likely not; if you flood a state with mules, you probably will not scare out any Ph.D.s, and vice versa. The causal link is most likely indirect, by way of some third variable that is causally related both to number of mules and to number of Ph.D.s—for example, a variable like degree of urbanization. Urban states undoubtedly have a greater number of attractive positions for Ph.D.s, and rural states have greater use for mules.[16]

Since it is not likely that society has deep and abiding beliefs about the relationship between mules and Ph.D.s, that relationship is not a likely candidate for the fallacy of inferring causation from association. Consider a relationship that does touch the prevailing system of beliefs, however: the relationship between one-parent families and juvenile delinquency, for example. From a study that shows the incidence of delinquency to be higher in one-parent families than in two-parent families, it is not unlikely that the one-parent family will appear to many as the cause of delinquency. Yet it is entirely possible that a third variable such as poverty may be the cause of both the one-parent family and juvenile delinquency when these phenomena occur together. But the investigator will not search for a third variable if he is satisfied with his findings. And this act of omission lends further credibility to the fallacious interpretation. Belief makes partial information seem like complete information. The point is that when an association between variables germane to social belief is found, there is a tendency to treat that association as if it were a causal relationship, and to search no further.

The social scientist does not, indeed cannot, completely divest himself of culturally imposed and vested interest-related concepts and view the world as if neither it nor he had been born until that moment. Like all people, his vision is colored by the filter of his already formed and interrelated conceptual system. And though he can discipline himself to withhold understanding, to prolong observation prior to imposing meaning on the phenomenon observed, the extent to which he can do this is limited, for cultural and personal interests frequently lie below the psychological sights, hence not accessible to conscious control.

It should be noted, too, that a theory is as precious to the theorist who conceived it as a child is to his mother. A person who has spent much of his life cultivating and elaborating a complex theoretical system is not likely, even when confronted by contradictory evidence, to make fundamental changes in this theory. We would be hard put, for example, to find two wholly different theories about the same phenomenon that were proposed by the same theorist. Faced with disparate sensory data, the theorist more than likely attempts to redefine the new and unnerving information to make it fit his system or, if this proves futile, he may account for the new information by building a theoretical annex onto his original structure. It is in recognition of the profound, multifaceted biasing effect of the theorist in the theory that Gouldner suggests the need for a reflexive sociology, a sociology that takes the sociologist into account.[17]

CRITERIA AND CAUTION

Given that social science theory is neither precise nor objective, that every set of human phenomena can be interpreted in many different ways, and that each interpretation is political both in content and consequence, it is imperative that the social worker exercise caution in the selection and use of explanatory theory. Before selecting any single explanation of a particular event, he should weigh the relative merit of alternative explanations in terms of two broad criteria: predictive value and philosophical compatibility. That is, the social worker must ask himself two

questions about each explanation he considers: Is it useful?
Should I use it?

According to Briar and Miller, "beyond the question of
validity, or the 'truth' of a theory, the test of a theory for the
practitioner is pragmatic: is it useful in meeting the tasks he
faces?" [18] And a theory is useful in a given situation to the
extent that it enables the social worker to predict and therefore exercise some measure of control over future events. For
example, the proposition that persons interact more frequently
with those seated across from them than with those seated
adjacent to them [19] is a useful piece of theory, for it enables
the worker to predict from observation of the seating arrangement which people at a given meeting are likely to engage each
other. Further, it provides a guide for worker intervention to
change the interaction pattern. Should the worker wish to
alter the flow of communication, he can modify the seating
arrangement.

Given that a particular theory is useful for its predictive
value in a particular situation, the second criterion, philosophical compatibility, must be applied; for not all social science
theory is compatible with the value structure of social work in
general and recent developments in professional valuation in
particular. And the interventive activity which theory predicated on unacceptable values and beliefs implies must be rejected as unacceptable social worker behavior. Consider, for
example, two different explanations of deviance phenomena.

Psychoanalytic theory locates the source of deviant behavior
(and all other behavior) inside the individual, emphasizing
internal determinants of personality presumably formed for all
time in early childhood. This denies the influence of present
situational factors, thereby precluding changes in the institutional context for behavior as a viable aim of social work intervention. It suggests that the social worker can, at best, help
people gain insight into the early sources of their current

behavior so that they may, with a huge expenditure of energy, slightly modify that behavior. Aside from the pessimism involved, the presupposition of psychic determinism in psychoanalytic theory blames the victim and absolves the present institutional arrangements of all responsibility. This is anathema to the values on which a structural approach to social work practice is predicated.

A theory that explains deviant behavior in terms of culturally imposed goals and differential access to means,[20] on the other hand, locates the problem in the social environment. This explanation emphasizes situational determinants and implies a need for change in the opportunity structure of society—an aim for interventive activity that *is* compatible with the values underlying a structural approach to social work.

Psychoanalytic theory should be rejected on the grounds of philosophical incompatibility. Similarly, theories which account for poverty in terms of lack of motivation among the poor should be rejected. And theories which explain low academic achievement and high unemployment rates among blacks in terms of biological inferiority and intellectual, moral, or cultural deprivation must all be rejected on the grounds of philosophical incompatibility.

It should be noted that the term "social science" generally includes sociology, social psychology, and psychology—three levels of analysis of human behavior. Sociology is concerned with organized patterns of collective behavior, the development, structure, and functions of human groups, and differences in human behavior as a function of group membership. The group or institution is the basic unit of analysis. Social psychology takes the individual as the basic unit of analysis and is concerned with social influences on individual behavior, that is, with external determinants. Psychology also takes the individual as the basic unit of analysis, but holds the environment constant in order to focus on individual mental processes, on internal determinants of individual behavior. In terms of the implications of social science theory for interventive activity, sociological and social-psychological explanations direct the practitioner to social structures, while psychological explanations direct intervention toward the internal, psychological processes of individuals. Therefore, sociological and social-psychological explanations tend to be more philosophically compatible with a structural approach to social work than do psychological explanations, and this accounts for the greater emphasis on sociological and social-psychological theory in the second part of this chapter.

In general, the social worker should view social science theories as tools for his use in the performance of his professional assignments. Like all users of tools, he should select the one that best fits the particular problem which confronts him at a given moment, and discard it when it no longer implements his task. Such an approach serves to minimize theoretical bias, while increasing the biasing effect of the value structure of the profession—as it should! This is not to suggest that unrestrained eclecticism is the ideal. Rather, as Briar and Miller indicate, the profession itself must "examine the tasks and realties confronting practitioners and . . . begin the laborious effort of *developing* theories suited to those tasks and realities." [21] Pieces of various theories should be "selected and evaluated in light of an explicit conception of the *mission* and *tasks*.[22] This puts social work "in charge of the shape and content of its knowledge base and does not delegate this responsibility to other disciplines." [23] This book is one effort to specify a mission and a set of tasks, and to suggest some of the many pieces of social science theory relevant to that mission and that set of tasks. Until the profession accomplishes this, however, eclecticism guided by the two criteria of predictive value and philosophical compatibility may be in order.

In any event, the social worker must studiously avoid hypostatization, the confusion of theory with external reality, by recognizing that the concepts he uses to explain a situation are not part of that situation. Rather, they are a set of categories into which he sorts out and thereby gives meaning to the phenomena comprising the situation. The concepts he uses are his own contribution to the situation. It follows logically from this that the social worker's selection of a particular theory to explain a particular event is a decision to contribute a certain set of concepts to that event, a set of concepts that shape the event in a particular way but not the only possible way. And to the extent that the social worker's contribution is consequential, he, not the theorist, is responsible for the consequences.

To aid the social worker to select theory relevant to a structural approach to practice, some propositions are presented in the next section. Because the proposition is the least complex unit of theory that specifies relationships among variables, presumably, the propositional form makes social science more accessible for at-the-moment use by practitioners to guide intervention. The propositions offered here are not accompanied by discussion since they are designed to suggest rather than elaborate some pertinent areas of inquiry. For further elaboration, readers are referred to the sources cited for that purpose.

RELEVANT PROPOSITIONS

SOCIAL INFLUENCE

In order to develop community action systems and/or help clients obtain their entitlement, the social worker needs to influence others (D-type activity). It follows that he needs to understand the nature and operation of social influence, the ability of one person to cause a change in the overt behavior

and/or private opinion of another person. This includes familiarity with different types of influence, the conditions under
which each is likely to succeed, and the probable consequences
for the worker-other relationship that use of each is likely to
produce. To this end, the following propositions are offered:

1. An individual tends to comply with the request of another
who provides relevant information or points out relevant contingencies of which he was unaware if, and only if, the content communicated is consistent with his value system.[24]

2. Where there is mutual attraction, an individual tends to
comply with the request of another who appeals to their similarity in the domain within which influence is attempted.[25]

3. An individual tends to comply with the request of another
whom he believes has the "right," by virtue of position or
role, to prescribe behavior for him.[26]

4. An indiviual tends to comply with the request of another
to whom he attributes superior knowledge or ability in the
domain within which influence is attempted if, and only if, he
trusts the motives of the other.[27]

5. An individual tends to comply with the request of another who can mediate punishments and rewards for him.[28]

6. In the instance of successful influence based on information, attraction, position, or expertise, compliance tends to
extend beyond overt behavior to private belief. In the instance
of successful influence based on reward or punishment, on the
other hand, compliance tends to be restricted to overt
behavior.[29]

7. In the instance of influence based on reward or punishment, effectiveness is a function of the continued presence of
the influencer. In the instance of influence based on information, attraction, position, or expertise, on the other hand, the
presence of the influencer is not relevant.[30]

8. Reward-based influence tends to produce positive atti-

tudes toward the influencer, while punishment-based influence
tends to produce negative attitudes toward the influencer.[31]

The social worker's potential to influence others in the service of his clients is not limited to the dyadic situation, however.
To the contrary, groups exert powerful forces on individual
members, and the worker who understands the conditions under which group pressure toward conformity operates has an
important tool at his disposal. He can either use the power of
the group to influence particular members, or he can reduce
the likelihood that the group will influence particular members
by altering the conditions that obtain. The following propositions pertain to conformity:

1. Group discussion tends to produce more attitude change
than do lectures or directives.[32]

2. An individual tends to conform to group opinion when
the object or event to be judged is ambiguous.[33]

3. An individual tends to conform to group opinion when
the group is cohesive.[34]

4. An individual tends to conform to group opinion when he
must make his opinion public if, and only if, he is highly at-
tracted to the group.[35]

5. An individual's tendency to conform to group opinion
increases as the size of the majority whose opinion differs from
his increases.[36]

6. An individual's tendency to conform to group opinion
decreases when the majority opinion is not unanimous.[37]

Other propositions that are potentially useful for the social
worker in his effort to influence others in the interest of his
clients include the following:

1. Where there are a number of roles which the other person could occupy, taking a complementary role tends to act as
a pressure on him to select one of them.[38]

2. When an individual does something for another, the other

tends to reciprocate by performing some equivalent act for him.[39]

GROUP BEHAVIOR

The social worker's effort to create client self-help networks (A-type activity) or to organize some clients into a unit for collective action in behalf of themselves and others (B-type activity) requires knowledge of the structures and dynamics of groups. Further, the worker's individual attempt to make his own and other social agencies more responsive to client need (D-type activity) must be grounded in a basic understanding of patterns of collective behavior. The following propositions are among those that seem pertinent:

1. In an initially leaderless group, the person who talks most usually emerges as the leader.[40]

2. People tend to talk more to those seated across from them than to those seated adjacent to them.[41]

3. In an initially leaderless group, the person who occupies the head of the table tends to emerge as the leader.[42]

4. When group members expect democratic leadership, democratic leadership tends to produce a more effective group than authoritarian leadership does. When group members expect authoritarian leadership, authoritarian leadership tends to produce a more effective group than democratic leadership does.[43]

5. Any movement of members from one position in the role structure to another, or any discrepancies in the criteria for establishing status, tends to result in efforts to reestablish the structure or resolve the differences, with a consequent decrease in group productivity.[44]

6. Group interaction with a deviant tends to increase when his deviancy is initially noticed and decrease when either he begins to conform or is judged "hopeless" by the other members and consequently rejected.[45]

7. Groups tend to retain a deviant member who has special skills which the group needs.[46]

8. As group size increases, the average contribution of each member decreases.[47]

9. When resources are differentially distributed in a three-person situation, there is a tendency for the two persons who control fewer resources to form a coalition if, and only if, the two persons together control more resources than the third person alone.[48]

10. When resources are differentially distributed in a situation involving four or more persons, a coalition tends to form in which the combined resources are the minimum amount necessary to determine the outcome of the decision.[49]

11. When the goals of one group are in conflict with the goals of another group so that each can achieve its ends only at the expense of the other, their members tend to become hostile to each other.[50]

12. Group cohesiveness tends to increase as antagonism to some other out-group increases.[51]

13. Attraction to the group tends to increase when a severe initiation precedes admission to membership.[52]

NONVERBAL BEHAVIOR

As the social worker talks with clients about contract formation or social action, as he talks with colleagues at staff meetings or in the corridors, as he talks with community representatives or professionals from related agencies or disciplines, he is engaged in a human exchange. This human exchange, the flow of affect from worker to other, is largely an unconscious process of implication and inference that occurs over, under, within, and around the deliberate verbal exchange of task-related information. And while it is more subtle than the exchange of task-related information, it is no less powerful with respect to the outcome, for it defines the relationship within which work on the task proceeds. To maximize the possibility of task accomplishment, the worker must consciously control his nonverbal behavior as well as his verbal behavior. He must deliberately select his postures and gestures in order to communicate the precise affective message he intends. To do this, the worker must be familiar with the affective value (positive vs. negative) of different nonverbal behaviors, and propositions of the following order may prove helpful.

1. Asymmetrical arm and leg positions (one arm akimbo and one free; one foot slightly in front of the other) tend to be associated with positive feeling, while symmetrical arm and leg positions (arms akimbo or crossed at chest; feet together) tend to be associated with negative feeling.[53]

2. Moderately open arm positions tend to be associated with positive feeling, while close arm positions tend to be associated with negative feeling.[54]

3. A slightly forward lean tends to be associated with positive feeling, while a backward lean tends to be associated with negative feeling.[55]

4. Moderately close distances tend to be associated with positive feeling, while extremely close and extremely far distances tend to be associated with negative feeling.[56]

5. Frequent eye contact tends to be associated with positive feeling, while staring or minimal eye contact tends to be associated with negative feeling.

6. Moderate volume and moderate pitch tend to be associated with positive feeling, while high volume and high pitch tend to be associated with negative feeling.[58]

7. Rapid speech rate and excessive gesticulation tend to be associated with negative feeling.[59]

8. Fidgeting (finger tapping, foot tapping) tends to be associated with negative feeling.[60]

TOWARD A THEORY FOR SOCIAL WORK

Although the suggested areas of inquiry and the specific propositions offered within each area are few in number, to have attempted more at this time would be both premature and beyond the scope of this book. The intent is to point a direction for continuing work on the important task that Briar and Miller [61] have defined. It seems reasonable to assume that identification of relevant propositions is the first step toward building a knowledge base for social work practice. The search for interrelatedness among propositions that culminates in a theory has to come later.

Chapter 13

Conclusion: Toward Effective Practice

In today's world no professional is immune from attacks from a vocal public, by professionals within his/her own ranks, and by others who wish to perform those acts previously reserved for the credentialed. The charges include: The professions have become established, institutionalized, and rigid. They have developed a mystique which defines their work as extremely complex, requiring extended education, great intelligence and skill, and highly sophisticated judgment that only other professionals in the same field are qualified to judge. They are controlled by a conservative old guard. They are responsible only to their colleagues, not to the people they serve.[1] Some even claim that nonprofessionals can do the jobs better. Social workers suffer these charges along with doctors, lawyers, teachers, and others—perhaps even more, for social work was never popular because of its association with the poor and economically burdensome. But the most serious charge that has been leveled at the social worker is that he is not effective. In some cases the charge is ill-founded, even ironic, as when members of the social work profession who by and large have not been the architects of our nation's social policies and programs are nevertheless attributed with, and discredited by, the failures. Frequently, however, the charge is not ill-founded. Effectiveness studies [2] provide ample evidence that the often-heard statement that social work is a helping profession speaks more to intent than to outcome. As Briar points out, we cannot ignore these findings. Nor can we conclude that the researchers studied the wrong variables or the wrong social workers.[3] Nor can we simply adopt theories and methods developed by other professions to suit their own unique tasks. Nor can we despair. The challenge is sobering.

Given that an instance of social work practice can be labeled "effective" if, and only if, the act or set of acts performed by the worker produces the desired outcome, it follows that the desired outcome must be clearly specified and stated in behavioral terms with observable referents. Without such precision in stating the goal, there is no way to measure the degree to which the result obtained approximates the result desired; hence there is no way to determine effectiveness. In other words, we have to be specific about our goals so that we can know if and when we have reached them. Moreover, without precise goals there are no criteria for differentiating relevant acts from irrelevant acts. Specific goals guide selection of relevant propositions which, in turn, suggest relevant acts to be performed in order to accomplish the goals (see Chapter 12). In essence, we have to know where we want to go before we can figure out how to get there. Mager summarized the need for precision in stating goals when he warned teachers, "if you're not sure where you're going, you're liable to end up someplace else—*and not even know it.*" [4]

Given a precise goal stated in behavioral terms, the next step on the path to effective practice is the selection of social science propositions that indicate what acts can be expected to produce that goal. The empirical proposition is the link between social science and effective social work practice. Practice principles are nothing more (and nothing less) than propositions coupled with values. A practice principle is a statement of what the worker *ought* to do or how he *ought* to do it. It is a directive or a guide for practice. Beyond principles, effective practice requires specification of behavior through which the principles can be applied in specific instances of practice. Effective practice flows from clear goals, relevant propositions translated into practice principles, and specific acts through which the principles can be applied and the goals accomplished.

In this book we described a structural model for microlevel social work practice. While the content of the model was shaped by a social-welfare-through-social-change philosophy, the challenge of effectiveness shaped its articulation. We tried to be specific, to explicate the model in terms of what to do and how to do it. We constructed a frame of reference defined by types of activity through which the model could be seen in relation to other forms of social work. We made our assumptions explicit, first, because the assumptions on which a model is predicated infuse the model with a particular value orientation; and second, because a model can be expected to hold only for situations that meet the assumptions underlying it. We identified a three-part professional assignment and elaborated four principles and ten procedures through which the principles can be applied in practice. We described four roles in terms of expectations for the content of behavior to be enacted at different times in accord with the principle of following the demands of the client task and the principle of least contest. We designated six areas of skill, articulating twenty-seven discrete behaviors and the conditions that occasion their use in terms of noises and gestures to be produced in response to noises and gestures produced by others. As we have indicated throughout the text, the job is by no means complete. Where further work seems indicated we have suggested the direction it might take.

Our focus continues to be on what the practitioner does, in

contrast to client response, out of the conviction that only as interventions can be described in specific terms (however difficult it is to capture action with words) can practitioners and researchers systematically collect outcome data that have meaning for practice, in the sense that it can tell us what produced the outcome observed so that we can use or not use that intervention depending on whether or not the outcome which that intervention can be expected to produce is the desired outcome. In so far as we were able to describe the model at a behavioral level, it is accessible to empirical study in the ordinary course of practice. The practice act is simultaneously a research act, and the worker can test his own practice as he practices it, using the results to modify and/or further develop the model. It is through this continuing process of building models, submitting them to inquiry, and rebuilding them that effective practice will emerge and be known as effective.

Report of Service to Client

The following episode illustrates one worker's use of some of the intervention behavior articulated in Chapters 7 through 10. The setting is Teen Center, an agency that provides, among other services, emergency housing (known as "crashing") for teenagers who have run away from home.

About 8:00 P.M. a young guy (looked about 15 or 16) with a knapsack walked into the office and looked around. "Hi," I said. *"What's up?"* "Hi," he said, turning toward me. "I need a place to crash." *I got up from behind the desk, sat down in a chair near some other chairs, and* asked him if he wanted to sit. He said, "Yeh, okay," took off his knapsack, dropped it and his jacket on one of the other chairs and sat down. *"Where you coming from?" I asked, pointing to the knapsack.* "I split from home," he said. "In Scranton. I couldn't hack it anymore." *I turned my chair so we were at right angles to each other* and asked, *"Your parents hassling you a lot?"* He said, "Yeh, especially my old man." He turned his face toward me, then looked away and said, in

←⎡Reaching for⎤
  ⎣information⎦

←⎡Positioning⎤

←⎡Reaching for⎤
  ⎣information⎦

←⎡Positioning⎤

←⎡Checking out an⎤
  ⎣inference⎦

a much softer, more hesitant voice, "He's in the bag half the time." *I said, "That can really get you down."* There was a long silence. *I waited.*

Reaching for feelings ←

Waiting out feelings ←

He rubbed his lips with his hand and shifted restlessly. He looked as though he were about to say something a few times, but he only sighed. Finally he broke the silence by saying that he was more than down. His lips were tight across his teeth and his voice was loud. He turned his head, and I could not see his face as he said, in the same loud, tight voice, "I'm pissed off." Then, more softly, "He beats the hell out of me." *"Wow," I said. "What a bust."* "No kidding," he said, looking at me. "That's why I split. I heard about this place from a friend of mine, so I thought I'd check it out. Can you get me a place to stay?" *I said, "Yeh, I think so, but I have to wait until 8:30 to get in touch with some folks. Did you eat?"* He shook his head "no." *I asked him if he wanted to,* and he shrugged his shoulders and said, "No bread." *I said it was on the house* and phoned out for sandwiches for both of us.

Attending ←

Getting with feelings ←

Providing information ←

Reaching for information ←

Providing information ←

When I got off the phone *I returned to the seat near him* and took out a cigarette. He pulled out a pad of matches and lit it for me. I said thanks and *asked him what I should call him.* He said his name was Anthony, then he laughed. *"What?" I asked.* "I was just thinking that I should have said Ishmael," he said. I laughed.

Positioning ←

Reaching for information ←

Reaching for information ←

I told him I was Fran, and after a few minutes of conversation about names I phoned the Murphys and told them to expect Anthony by 10:00. *I wrote down the address and directions for getting there (walking distance) and gave it to him.* He

Providing information ←

Providing information ←

thanked me and I nodded. *I told him they would put him up for three nights if he wanted, but that three nights was all that Teen Center could provide.* He said it was okay.

← [Providing information]

The food came, and while we were eating *I asked Anthony what happens when he leaves the Murphys.* He said he wasn't sure, that maybe he could get some kind of job somewhere, helping out on a farm maybe. He said he's got a better chance in a farm area than in the city where everybody cares more about his age than what he can do. *"You tried in the city,"* I said. "Yeh," he said, "I tried." He shook his head from side to side and said they wouldn't even let him pump gas. He said he wasn't kidding himself, that he never thought it would be easy, but that if he could just survive for the next three and a half years he'll be eighteen; he'll be able to get a city job and go to night school. "You know what I want to be?" he asked. *"What?" I asked.* "A doctor," he said. Then he looked at me and laughed. *"What?" I asked.* "It's a lousy way to start a medical career, isn't it," he said. *"Yeh," I said, nodding.* Then there was silence. Again, *I waited.*

← [Reaching for information]

← [Attending]

← [Checking out an inference]

← [Attending]

← [Reaching for information]

← [Reaching for information]

← [Getting with feelings]

← [Waiting out feelings]

Anthony broke the silence with an angry statement that every time he thinks about later he could kill that bastard. He said it would all be so easy if he could have stayed home like everyone else. *"It's a bummer," I said.* He nodded. Then he announced in a sarcastic tone of voice, "You know I'll never be a doctor, don't you?" Then, "Aren't you going to tell me I ought to go home and finish school?" *"Is that what you'd like to do?" I asked.* He pressed his

← [Getting with feelings]

← [Checking out an inference]

lips tightly together and looked away. *I waited.*   ←⎡Waiting out feelings⎤

When he turned toward me again he said I wouldn't believe what it was like. *"What was it like?" I asked.* He said that   ←⎡Reaching for information⎤

nothing he did was right, that he took too long getting home from school, or his room was messy, or he was sitting in the wrong   ←⎡Attending⎤

chair or keeping the light on too late or moving around too early. He said that everything bothered his father, that sometimes his father would even come after him for not looking at him. *"Just you?" I asked.*   ←⎡Reaching for information⎤

"My sister, too," he said. "She split right away." *"What do you mean right away?"*   ←⎡Reaching for information⎤

I asked. He said it was about a year ago, that he was never too crazy about his   ←⎡Attending⎤

father, but that about a year ago it started to get worse. He said his father stopped going to work and was stoned most of the time. He said the beatings started and his sister cut out. *I asked him what about*   ←⎡Reaching for information⎤

his mother, and he said that his father doesn't touch her. *I asked him what his*   ←⎡Reaching for information⎤

mother did when his father came after him or his sister, and he said she would try to calm him down, that sometimes she could get him to stop, but sometimes she couldn't, and that lately she couldn't   ←⎡Attending⎤

seem to stop him at all. He said she would tell him that his father was sick and that he should try to understand. He said that once he told his mother that the old man should see a shrink, but she said no, that his father wasn't crazy and that he shouldn't mention it again. *"Then your*   ←⎡Checking out an inference⎤

family wasn't trying to get any outside help?" I asked. He said he didn't think so, that his mother figured it was just a matter of time and everything would be

okay. *"But you don't think so,"* I said.   ←⎡Checking out an⎤
He said he didn't know, that maybe she   ⎣inference   ⎦
was right, but that he couldn't stick around
to find out. "I just can't let him beat me
any more," he said in a high-pitched voice.
"Yeh," I said, *nodding.* "It's a bitch," he   ←⎡Getting with⎤
said. *I nodded again.* Then *I asked, "Am I*   ←⎣feelings   ⎦
right that you'd want to live at home and   ←⎡Checking out an⎤
go to school if there were some way to keep   ⎣inference   ⎦
your father from beating you?" "You know
it," he said, but added that there was no
way because his father was bigger and
stronger than he. Then he raised his eye-
brows and said, "Unless there was a way
to get *him* out of the house." *"Oh?"* I   ←⎡Reaching for⎤
asked. "Ya," he said. "Like a hospital or   ⎣information ⎦
something." *I said that might be a way, or*   ←⎡Providing   ⎤
there may be other ways to keep his father   ⎣information ⎦
from beating him, that it sounded to me
like he needed some help from someone in
Scranton who could look into the situation
and see what might be possible. I said that
maybe one of the child welfare workers
could help. He asked me if he would have
to go back before the welfare people
would do anything, and *I said I didn't*   ←⎡Providing   ⎤
know, but that if he wanted me to I could   ⎣information ⎦
call up and explore it for him tomorrow.
"Ya," he said with enthusiasm; "That
would be great." *I said that I wasn't prom-*   ←⎡Providing   ⎤
ising anything, that maybe they wouldn't   ⎣information ⎦
be able to help, but that at least we'd know
a little more than we do now. He said he
understood. Then *I said that if the child*   ←⎡Pointing out ⎤
welfare people got into it his mother might   ⎢a possible   ⎥
not like it. "Ya," he said. "I forgot about   ⎣consequence⎦
that. . . . Maybe you better not call them."
There were a few moments of silence, and
then *I said, "Look, Anthony, you don't*
have to make a decision tonight. It's get-

ting late anyhow and you have to get to the
Murphy's by 10:00. We can talk more
about it tomorrow if you want. He thought
that was a good idea because he needed
time to think, and we agreed on early
afternoon.

←⎡ Providing   ⎤
　⎣ information ⎦

Notes

CHAPTER 1: INTRODUCTION

1. Herbert J. Gans, "The New Egalitarianism," *Saturday Review,* May 6, 1972, pp. 43–46.

2. The implications of this perspective in terms of planning and offering social services are elaborated by Charles F. Grosser, "Changing Theory and Changing Practice," *Social Casework,* VIIIL, No. 1 (1967), 16–21.

3. Charlotte Towle, "Social Work: Cause and Function," *Social Casework,* XLII, No. 8 (1961), 385–97.

4. Murray Levine and Adeline Levine, *A Social History of Helping Services* (New York: Appleton-Century-Crofts, 1970), p. 8.

5. For an earlier discussion, see Nathan E. Cohen, *Social Work in the American Tradition* (New York: Holt, Rinehart, and Winston, 1958).

6. Lawrence A. Cremin, *The Transformation of the School* (New York: Alfred A. Knopf, 1961), pp. 345–53.

7. Levine and Levine, *op. cit.*

8. Mary Richmond, *What Is Social Case Work?* (New York: Russell Sage Foundation, 1922), pp. 224 and 225.

9. Barbara Wootton, *Social Science and Social Pathology* (London: Allen and Unwin, 1959), p. 286.

10. Charlotte Towle, "New Developments in Social Casework in the United States," *British Journal of Psychiatric Social Work,* Vol. I, No. 2 (1955).

11. Charlotte Towle, "Social Casework in Modern Society," *Social Service Review,* XX, No. 2 (1946), 175.

12. Bertha C. Reynolds, "Social Case Work: What Is It? What Is Its Place in the World Today?" *The Family,* XVI (1935), 238.

13. Lela B. Costin, "A Historical Review of School Social Work," *Social Casework*, L, No. 8 (1969), 439–453.

14. Wootton, *op. cit.*, p. 295.

15. Grosser, *op. cit.*, elaborates this viewpoint and distinguishes it from a pathology viewpoint.

CHAPTER 2: A FRAME OF REFERENCE FOR
SOCIAL WORK PRACTICE

1. The type of research suggested here is descriptive only; hence the findings will function like a road map, illustrating where things are in relation to each other. The driver will decide, based on criteria external to the map, where to go and which route to take. It should be noted, too, that even an evaluative study that reveals route X to be more effective (shorter, safer) than route Y does not, in and of itself, say "Use $X!$" although presumably the study was conducted for the purpose of making such a decision. The point is that research measures; it does not command.

CHAPTER 3: ASSUMPTIONS, ASSIGNMENT, AND
AREAS OF SPECIALIZATION

1. For further discussion of this issue see William Ryan, *Blaming the Victim* (New York: Pantheon Books, 1971).

2. For further discussion of the concepts of "social problem" and "social task" see Eliot Studt, *A Conceptual Approach to Teaching Materials* (New York: Council on Social Work Education, 1965).

3. For an example of this see Francis Purcell and Harry Specht, "The House on Sixth Street," *Social Work*, X, No. 4 (1965), 69–76.

CHAPTER 4: BASIC PRINCIPLES OF A
STRUCTURAL APPROACH TO PRACTICE

1. See Florence Hollis, *Casework: a Psychosocial Therapy* (New York: Random House, 1964); Elizabeth McBroom, "Socialization and Social Casework," pp. 313–51, and Edwin J. Thomas, "Behavioral Modification and Casework," pp. 181–218, in Robert W. Roberts and Robert H. Nee, eds., *Theories of Social Casework.* (Chicago: University of Chicago Press, 1970); Robert D. Vinter, "The Essential Components of Social Group

Work Practice," in Robert D. Vinter, ed., *Readings in Group Work Practice* (Ann Arbor, Mich.: Campus Publishers, 1967), pp. 3–8.

2. See William Schwartz, "The Social Worker in the Group," in *New Perspectives on Services to Groups* (New York: National Association of Social Workers, 1961), pp. 7–29; Virginia Satir, *Conjoint Family Therapy* (rev. ed.; Palo Alto, Calif.: Science and Behavior Books, Inc., 1967).

3. Martin Rein, "The Social Service Crisis: the Dilemma—Success for the Agency or Service for the Needy?" *Trans-action,* I, No. 5 (1964), 3–8.

4. Peter M. Blau, *The Dynamics of Bureaucracy,* (Chicago: University of Chicago Press, 1955).

CHAPTER 5: SOCIAL WORK ROLES

1. Lillian D. Wald,   *The House on Henry Street* (New York: Holt, Rinehart, and Winston, 1915).

2. Jane Addams, *Twenty Years at Hull-House* (New York: Macmillan Co., 1910).

3. Jacob Riis, *How the Other Half Lives* (New York: Scribner's, 1917).

4. Robert Perlman and David Jones, *Neighborhood Service Centers* (Washington, D.C.: U.S. Department of Health, Education, and Welfare, Office of Juvenile Delinquency and Youth Development, 1967), pp. 12–15.

5. Nathan E. Cohen, ed., *Social Work and Social Problems* (New York: National Association of Social Workers, 1964); Scott Briar, "The Social Worker's Responsibility for the Civil Rights of Clients," *New Perspectives,* I, No. 1 (1967), 89–92; George A. Brager, "Advocacy and Political Behavior," *Social Work,* XIII, No. 2 (1968), 5–15; *Ad Hoc* Committee on Advocacy, "The Social Worker as Advocate: Champion of Social Victims," *Social Work,* XIV, No. 2 (1969), 16–22; Willard C. Richan and Marvin Rosenberg, *The Advo-Kit* (copyright Richan and Rosenberg, 1971).

6. Willard C. Richan, "The Public Welfare Worker—Advocate or Adversary," presented at Northeast Regional Conference of the American Public Welfare Association, 1970.

7. Willard C. Richan, "Presto: You Are a Social Work Advocate," p. 15; presented at Eastern Regional Institute, National Association of Social Workers, 1969.

8. Theodore R. Sarbin, "Notes on the Transformation of Social Identity," in Lehigh M. Roberts, Norman S. Greenfield, and Milton H. Millers, eds., *Comprehensive Mental Health: the Challenge of Evaluation* (Madison, Wis.: University of Wisconsin Press, 1968), pp. 97–115.

9. Robert K. Merton, *Social Theory and Social Structure* (Glencoe, Ill.: Free Press, 1957); Robert Rosenthal, "Self-fulfilling Prophecy," *Psychology Today,* II, No. 4 (1968), 46–51.

10. Richan and Rosenberg, *op. cit.,* p. 1.

11. Erving Goffman, "On Cooling the Mark Out: Some Aspects of Adaptation to Failure," *Psychiatry,* XV (1952), 451–63.

12. William Schwartz, "The Social Worker in the Group," in *New Perspectives on Services to Groups* (New York: National Association of Social Workers, 1961), pp. 7–29; William Schwartz and Serapio Zalba, eds., *The Practice of Group Work* (New York: Columbia University Press, 1971).

13. Peter Kropotkin, *Mutual Aid: a Factor of Evolution* (New York: Alfred Knopf, 1925).

14. Schwartz, *op. cit.,* p. 17.

15. This list of expectations partially derives from the work of Schwartz, *ibid.*

16. For a fuller description of this and other ulterior motives that stand as obstacles to satisfactory relatedness to others see Eric Berne, *Games People Play* (New York: Grove Press, 1964).

17. Wald, *op. cit.;* Murray Levine and Adeline Levine, *A Social History of Helping Services* (New York: Appleton-Century-Crofts, 1970), Chaps. 5–6.

18. Scott Briar and Henry Miller, *Problems and Issues in Social Casework* (New York: Columbia University Press, 1971), pp. 3–31; Brian J. Heraud, *Sociology and Social Work* (Oxford, England: Pergamon Press, 1970), pp. 5–6.

19. Briar and Miller, *op. cit.,* pp. 237–40, provide an interesting example of a social worker in a mobile trailer serving the diverse needs of San Francisco's skid row population and outline the complex requirements of this role.

20. William Ryan, *Blaming the Victim* (New York: Pantheon Books, 1971). 1971.

CHAPTER 6: INTRODUCTION TO SKILL

1. Harold Lewis, "Developing a Program Responsive to New Knowledge and Values," in Edward J. Mullen and James R. Dumpson, eds., *Evaluation of Social Intervention* (San Francisco: Jossey-Bass, 1972), pp. 71–89.

2. Scott Briar and Henry Miller, *Problems and Issues in Social Casework* (New York: Columbia University Press, 1971), p. 184.

3. Michael Argyle, *The Psychology of Interpersonal Behavior* (Baltimore: Pelican, 1967).

4. Several behaviors that appear on this list were initially noted by Lawrence Shulman in *A Casebook of Social Work with Groups: the Mediating Model* (New York: Council on Social Work Education, 1968).

5. This approach to the concept skill differs from the more common usage having to do with proficiency in the performance of an act, (swimming, writing, lecturing). In general, references to skill in the social work literature are consistent with the common usage of the term. Implicit in such phrases as "skill in the use of a method" and "skill in the use of one's self" is a definition of skill as a degree of mastery. In fact, a basic approach to professional training emphasized practicing practice—an approach that presumes that the degree of mastery increases with repetition followed by examination of a written account of the performance with a supervisor. It should be noted, however, that the acts, such as swimming and use of one's self, to which the more common usage of the word "skill" is applied, are actually sets of smaller acts. Swimming includes arm and leg movements, head movements, breathing patterns, and so forth; use of one's self involves many of the specific behaviors listed. It seems reasonable to assume that smaller acts, however, leave less room for degrees of mastery in performance. That is to say, at some point there is a set of minute movements, each of which is either performed or not performed. As the number of movements involved in an act increases, on the other hand, some movements may be performed while other movements are not performed, resulting in some degree of mastery.

6. The authors are indebted to Harold Lewis for his thoughts regarding the place of analogues in the analytic process.

7. Erving Goffman, "On Cooling the Mark Out: Some Aspects of Adaptation to Failure," *Psychiatry*, XV (1952), 451–63.

8. Thomas Szasz, *The Myth of Mental Illness* (New York: Harper and Row, 1964).

CHAPTER 7: SKILL IN STAGE SETTING AND ATTENDING

1. See Erving Goffman, *The Presentation of Self in Everyday Life* (Garden City, N.Y.: Doubleday, 1959).

2. Edward T. Hall, "A System for the Notation of Proxemic Behavior," *American Anthropologist*, XLV (1963), 1003–26.

3. Kenneth B. Little, "Personal Space," *Journal of Experimental Social Psychology*, I (1965), 37–64; Robert Sommer, *Personal Space: the Behavioral Basis of Design* (Englewood Cliffs, N.J.: Prentice-Hall, Inc., 1969).

4. Dale F. Lott and Robert Sommer, "Seating Arrangements and Status," *Journal of Personality and Social Psychology*, VII (1967), 90–95.

5. Michael Argyle, *The Psychology of Interpersonal Behavior* (Baltimore: Pelican, 1967), p. 32; Albert E. Scheflen, "Stream and Structure of Communicational Behavior," Commonwealth of Pennsylvania, Eastern Pennsylvania Psychiatric Institute, Behavioral Studies; monograph 1 (1965).

6. Lott and Sommer, *op. cit.;* Paul Hare and Robert Bales, "Seating Position and Small Group Interaction," *Sociometry,* XXVI (1963), 480–86.

7. Robert K. Myers, "Some Effects of Seating Arrangements in Counseling," doctoral dissertation, University of Florida, Gainsville, 1969.

8. Sommer, *op. cit.*

9. Hall, *op. cit.,* p. 1009.

10. Argyle, *op. cit.,* p. 108.

11. Adam Kendon, "Some Functions of Gaze Direction in Social Interaction," *Acta Psychologica,* XXVI, No. 1 (1967) 1–47.

12. Hall, *op. cit.*

13. Lott and Sommer, *op. cit.;* Hare and Bales, *op. cit.;* Bernard M. Bass and Stanley Kluback, "Effects of Seating Arrangements on Leaderless Group Discussions," *Journal of Abnormal and Social Psychology,* XLVII (1952), 724–27; Lloyd T. Howells and Selwyn W. Becker, "Seating Arrangements and Leadership Emergence," *ibid.,* LXIV (1962), 148–50.

14. Ruth R. Middleman, *The Non-verbal Method in Working with Groups* (New York: Association Press, 1968).

15. Albert E. Scheflen, "Human Communication: Behavioral Programs and Their Integration," *Behavioral Science,* XIII, No. 1 (1968), 44–55, and "Non-language Behavior in Communication," presented at New York Chapter of the American Academy of Pediatrics, 1969.

16. The authors acknowledge Harold Lewis's discussion of analogues in his unpublished manuscript, "The Inner-directed Professional Question: Knowledge, Values, and Action in Social Work," Hunter College School of Social Work, 1971, pp. 125–30.

17. Lewis discusses internal professional questions and poses: "What am I to do now?" "How am I to act in this situation?" *Ibid.,* p. 8.

18. Gale Goldberg and Ruth R. Middleman, "It Might Be a Boa Constrictor Digesting an Elephant: Vision Stretching in Social Work Education," presented at 19th Annual Program Meeting, Council on Social Work Education, 1973; mimeographed.

19. For further discussion of social interaction skills see Argyle, *op. cit.,* pp. 86–96.

20. This behavior, reporting one's own feelings, is further elaborated in Chapter 8.

21. For other concepts related to following the other see "focused listening" in Allen E. Ivey, *Microcounseling* (Springfield, Ill.: Charles C.

Thomas, 1971), p. 57; also, "active listening," a concept elaborated by Thomas Gordon, *Parent Effectiveness Training: the No-lose Program for Raising Responsible Children* (New York: Wyden, 1970).

22. See Ivey, *op. cit.*, pp. 56–57 and 152–53, for a description of the skill "minimal encourages to talk" for further details on these types of cues. The major point of this skill is to show interest and involvement but to allow the client to determine the primary direction of the interview, through use of "um-hum," one-word questions, facial expressions, or repeating one or two words the client just said.

23. Incongruent communication in which the verbal and nonverbal segments of the message convey opposite meanings, the double-bind, is a concept that must be credited to Gregory Bateson and has been discussed extensively in the literature on human communication. In double-bind instances there is no way out if one were to follow both messages. See Jurgen Ruesch and Gregory Bateson, *Communication: the Social Matrix of Society* (New York: Norton, 1951); Paul Watzlawick, Janet Beavin, and Don Jackson, *The Pragmatics of Human Communication* (New York: Norton, 1967).

24. Michael M. Reese and Robert N. Whitman, "Expressive Movements, Warmth and Verbal Reinforcement," *Journal of Abnormal and Social Psychology*, LXIV (1962), 254–86. For other indicators of positive emotion see Chapter 8.

CHAPTER 8: SKILL IN ENGAGING FEELINGS

1. For the names of the first three behaviors the authors are indebted to Lawrence Shulman, *A Casebook of Social Work with Groups: the Mediating Model* (New York: Council on Social Work Education, 1968).

2. *ibid.*

3. Lawrence Shulman, "Social Work Skill: the Anatomy of a Helping Act," in *Social Work Practice, 1969* (New York: Columbia University Press, 1969), pp. 40–41.

4. Shulman, *A Casebook of Social Work with Groups.*

5. For theory and research on the "punctuation" function of nonverbal behavior see Albert E. Scheflen, "The Significance of Posture in Communication Systems," *Psychiatry*, XXVII (1964) 316–31.

6. For elaboration of the related concept, containment, see Helen U. Phillips, *Essentials of Social Group Work Skill* (New York: Association Press, 1957).

7. Carl Rogers, *Client-centered Therapy* (Boston: Houghton-Mifflin Co., 1951).

CHAPTER 9: SKILL IN ENGAGING INFORMATION

1. See the discussion of "open invitation to talk" in Allen E. Ivey, *Microcounseling* (Springfield, Ill.: Charles C. Thomas, 1971).

2. Lawrence Shulman, *A Casebook of Social Work with Groups: the Mediating Model* (New York: Council on Social Work Education, 1968).

3. William Schwartz, "The Social Worker in the Group," in *New Perspectives on Services to Groups* (New York: National Association of Social Workers, 1961), pp. 7–29.

4. For a related behavior, "helping the client to see his problem in a new way," see Shulman, *op. cit.;* see also Irwin Golden, "Teaching a Model of Group Work Skill: a Field Instructor's Report," in *Education for Social Work*, II, No. 4 (1966), 30–39.

CHAPTER 10: SKILL IN MANAGING INTERACTION AND ENGAGING BARRIERS

1. For further discussion of communication at the organismic and social levels, see Albert E. Scheflen, "On the Structuring of Human Communication," *American Behavioral Scientist*, I, No. 5 (1967), 8–12.

2. This view of language as controlling thought and action was proposed by Benjamin L. Whorf, *Language, Thought, and Reality* (Cambridge, Mass.: Massachusetts Institute of Technology Press, 1956), pp. 134–59.

3. Virginia Satir, *Conjoint Family Therapy* (rev. ed.: Palo Alto, Calif.: Science and Behavior Books, Inc., 1967), p. 70.

4. Norbert Wiener, *Cybernetics; or Control and Communication in the Animal and the Machine* (Cambridge, Mass.: Massachusetts Institute of Technology Press, 1948), and *The Human Use of Human Beings: Cybernetics and Society* (Boston: Houghton Mifflin, Co., 1950), adapts information theory and feedback mechanisms from mechanical to human terms. Information about the effect of one's communication is noticed by watching the other's reactions, which provide new information to the sender. Through this reprocessing in the brain of one's effect upon others (the feedback loop), the person adjusts his own next communication to keep it on target. These tiny, continuous adjustments may come from signals that say "keep on, you are being heard," or "slow down, you're too fast, too loud, etc." But the individual cannot always adapt himself to the requirements of a given situation. His interpretive mechanism may miss cues or may not respond to some that are noted out of other, more pressing needs of his own. In such instances the social worker gives the

feedback and thus interferes with the communication control processes of the sender of the message.

5. For a related concept, see stepping up weak signals in Lawrence Shulman, *A Casebook of Social Work with Groups* (New York: Council on Social Work Education, (1968), p. 79.

6. Mehrabian terms such cues subtle because they lack formal, organized ways to deal with them (dictionaries, agreed-upon coding, rules for syntax and grammar) in contrast to words. In other words, these behaviors remain subtle for us, not because they are less powerful than words, but because we know less about their function and usage. For further discussion of "implicit" and "explicit" aspects of language see Albert Mehrabian, *Nonverbal Communication* (Chicago: Aldine-Atherton, 1972), Chap. 1.

7. Jurgen Ruesch and Gregory Bateson, *Communication: the Social Matrix of Society* (New York: Norton, 1951).

8. A similar concept, stepping down a strong signal, is presented by Shulman, *op. cit.,* p. 79.

9. Shulman, *op. cit.,* p 80, refers to this behavior as "redirecting signal to actual intended recipient."

10. For further elaboration refer to discussion of "Courtroom" in Eric Berne, *Games People Play* (New York: Grove Press, Inc., 1964), pp. 96–98.

11. For the names of the second and fourth behaviors the authors are indebted to Shulman, *op. cit.*

12. *Ibid.*

13. Lawrence Shulman, "Social Work Skill: the Anatomy of a Helping Act," in *Social Work Practice, 1969* (New York: Columbia University Press, 1969), pp. 29–48.

14. Shulman, *A Casebook of Social Work with Groups.*

CHAPTER 11: THE METAWORK AND
THE ORGANIZATIONAL CONTEXT

1. John G. Hill and Ralph Ormsby, "The Philadelphia Time-Cost Study in Family Service," in *The Social Welfare Forum, 1953* (New York: Columbia University Press, 1953), pp. 205–26.

2. *Ibid.,* p. 222.

3. *Ibid.,* p. 220.

4. *Ibid.,* p. 221; emphasis added.

5. "Unit Cost Study," St. Louis, 1958; "Time Cost Study," Lycoming Co., Williamsport, Pa. and Children's Aid Society of Pennsylvania, 1961;

"Cost-Time Study for Family Counseling Agencies," New Jersey Council of Family Agencies, 1961; "Time Study of Total Staff," Decatur, Ill., 1962; "A Time and Cost Analysis of the Program of the Family Service Society," Salt Lake City, 1965; "Time Study," Edmonton, Alta., Canada, 1965; "Cost Analysis," Canton, Ohio, 1967, in *Research and Study Proposals of Family Service Society of America Member Organizations.*

6. Livia Lowy, *Time Utilization in Fifty FSAA Member Agencies* (New York: Family Service Association of America, 1971).

7. Direct-service time is equally encumbered in the public agencies. For example, time study averages for caseworkers' involvement with clients in eight districts of a public assistance agency (August, 1968) revealed 17.9 percent spent in the field (inclusive of travel time). The workers averaged 1.7 contacts with clients per day with 45.3 minutes spent per contact.

8. Scott Briar and Henry Miller, *Problems and Issues in Social Casework* (New York: Columbia University Press, 1971), pp. 144–45.

9. According to the FSAA report, Lowy, *op. cit.,* twenty-seven minutes of clerical time were needed to support one professional working hour. The services of one full-time clerical person were needed for every two equivalent full-time professional and administrative employees.

10. This estimate was made from the clerk-typist job specifications of the Philadelphia County Board of Assistance, DPW 8600 Ratings, July 10, 1963.

11. Briar and Miller, *op. cit.,* p. 144.

12. For further discussion of games workers and supervisors play see Alfred Kadushin, "Games People Play in Supervision," *Social Work,* XIII, No. 3 (1968), 23–32. Kadushin discusses many games that grow out of the anxieties generated by a situation in which the worker is expected to undergo change. See especially "Treat Me, Don't Beat Me," a game in which the worker exposes his self rather than his work, and the social worker part of the supervisor wants to respond.

13. For an elaborated discussion of the bases of power and social influence see Bertram H. Raven and Arie W. Kruglanski, "Conflict and Power," in Paul Swingle, ed., *The Structure of Conflict* (New York: Academic Press, 1970), pp. 69–109.

14. Erving Goffman, *The Presentation of Self in Everyday Life* (Garden City, N.Y.: Doubleday, 1959), p. 253.

15. Brian J. Heraud cites pertinent organizational research on this point. *Sociology and Social Work* (Oxford, England: Pergamon Press, 1970), p. 239.

16. For a summary of this literature see Archie Hanlan, "Changing Functions and Structures," pp. 39–50, Alfred J. Kutzik, "Class and Ethnic Factors," pp. 85–114, and Florence W. Kaslow, "Group Supervision,"

pp. 115–41, in Florence W. Kaslow *et al.*, *Issues in Human Services* (San Francisco: Jossey-Bass, 1972).

17. Lucille N. Austin, "An Evaluation of Supervision," *Social Casework*, XXXVII (1956), 375–82.

18. Hanlan, *op. cit.*

19. See, for example, Charles S. Levy, "The Ethics of Supervision," *Social Work*, XVIII, No. 2 (1973), 14–22; Betty Mandell, "The 'Equality' Revolution and Supervision," *Journal of Education for Social Work*, IX, No. 1 (1973), 43–55; Laura Epstein, "Is Autonomous Practice Possible?" *Social Work*, XVIII, No. 2 (1973), 5–12; Ruth R. Middleman, "Social Work Education: the Myth of the Agency as Partner," in *The Social Welfare Forum, 1973* (New York: Columbia University Press, 1974).

20. Edward E. Schwartz and William C. Sample, *The Midway Office* (New York: National Association of Social Workers, 1972).

21. Thomas Briggs, "Social Work Manpower Developments and Dilemmas of the 1970's," Workshops on Training MSW Students to Work with Various Categories of Social Welfare Personnel, Council on Social Work Education, Syracuse University, April, 1972.

22. See, for example, Rensis Likert, *The Human Organization: Its Management and Value* (New York: McGraw-Hill Book Co., 1967).

23. For example, L. L. Cummings and W. E. Scott, *Readings in Organizational Behavior and Human Performance* (Homewood, Ill.: Richard D. Irwin, Inc., and the Dorsey Press, 1969); Amitai Etzioni, *The Semi-Professions and Their Organization* (New York: Free Press, 1969); Likert, *op. cit.;* James G. March, ed., *Handbook of Organizations* (New York: Rand McNally, 1970); Heraud, *op. cit.*, Chaps. 10 and 11; Kaslow, *op. cit.*

24. C. Wright Mills, *The Sociological Imagination* (New York: Oxford University Press, 1959); Eliot Studt, *A Conceptual Approach to Teaching Materials* (New York: Council on Social Work Education, 1965).

25. Heraud, *op. cit.*

26. For a succinct overview of the orientations of several theorists (Barnard-Simon, Levinson, Mayo, Likert, Argyris, Blake, Shepard, McGregor, Leavitt, Thompson, and Tuden) and their key differences, see Warren G. Bennis, "Organizational Developments and the Fate of Bureaucracy," in Cummings and Scott, *op. cit.*, pp. 434–49.

27. *Ibid.*, pp. 444–48. For a discussion of the linking-pin concept see Rensis Likert, *New Patterns of Management* (New York: McGraw-Hill Book Co., 1961).

28. For full discussion of levels of analysis see Paul Lazarsfeld and Herbert Menzel, "On the Relation between Individual and Collective Properties," in Amitai Etzioni, ed., *A Sociological Reader* (New York: Holt, Rinehart, and Winston, 1961), pp. 499–516.

29. Douglas McGregor conceptualized two managerial styles: Theory *X* leaders believe that others avoid responsibility and work and are productive only when coerced by outside forces, while Theory *Y* leaders assume man is self-directing and if left to his own devices, will seek work and responsibility.

30. Abraham Maslow, *Eupsychian Management* (Homewood, Ill.: Richard D. Irwin, Inc., and the Dorsey Press, 1965).

31. Abraham Maslow, *Motivation and Personality* (2nd ed.; New York: Harper and Row, 1970).

32. Schwartz and Sample, *op. cit.*

CHAPTER 12: SOCIAL SCIENCE AND
SOCIAL WORK PRACTICE

1. *Society Today* (Del Mar, Calif.: Communications Research Machines, Inc., 1971), pp. 539–40.

2. Brian J. Heraud, *Sociology and Social Work* (New York: Pergamon Press, 1970), p. 14; emphasis added.

3. Alvin W. Gouldner, *The Coming Crisis of Western Sociology* (New York: Basic Books, 1970), p. 32.

4. Piaget elaborated such physically determined concepts as the concept of "object constancy" and the concept of "conservation of matter." See Hans G. Furth, *Piaget and Knowledge* (Englewood Cliffs, N.J.: Prentice-Hall, Inc., 1969).

5. Jerome S. Bruner, Jacqueline J. Goodnow, and George A. Austin, *A Study of Thinking* (New York: John Wiley and Sons, Inc., 1956), p. 10.

6. Harold C. Conklin, "The Relation of Hanunoo Culture to the Plant World," doctoral dissertation, Yale University, 1954.

7. Dorothy D. Lee, "Conceptual Implications of the Indian Language," *Philosophy of Science*, V (1938), 89–102.

8. Stanley S. Stevens, "Psychology: the Propaedeutic Science," *Philosophy of Science*, III, 1936), 93.

9. Gouldner, *op. cit.*

10. Parsons was born in 1902 and joined the faculty of the heavily endowed Harvard University in 1927. Thus he was too young to be personally affected by the First World War; he was a young adult during the prosperity of the 1920s; and he was already safe at Harvard prior to, and therefore not personally touched by, the depression years. For details, see Gouldner, *op. cit.*

11. George H. Mead, *Mind, Self and Society* (Chicago: University of Chicago Press, 1934).

12. John H. Van Evrie, *White Supremacy and Negro Subordination* (New York: Van Evrie, Horton, and Co., 1870).

13. Daniel P. Moynihan, *The Negro Family: the Case for National Action* (Washington, D.C.: U.S. Department of Labor, U.S. Government Printing Office, 1965).

14. Arthur Jensen, "How Much Can We Boost I.Q. and Scholastic Achievement?" *Harvard Educational Review*, XXXIX, No. 1 (1969), 1–123.

15. Rhett S. Jones, "Proving Blacks Inferior: 1870–1930," *Black World*, February, 1971, pp. 16–17.

16. Barry F. Anderson, *The Psychology Experiment* (Belmont, Calif.: Brooks and Cole Publishing Co., 1966), p. 9.

17. Gouldner, *op. cit.*

18. Scott Briar and Henry Miller, *Problems and Issues in Social Casework* (New York: Columbia University Press, 1971), p. 116.

19. Bernard Steinzor, "The Spatial Factor in Face-to-Face Discussion Groups," *Journal of Abnormal and Social Psychology*, XLV, (1950), 552–55.

20. Robert K. Merton, *Social Theory and Social Structure* (Glencoe, Ill.: Free Press, 1957).

21. Briar and Miller, *op. cit.*, p. 77.

22. *Ibid.*, p. 78; emphasis added.

23. *Ibid.*

24. The use of information to obtain compliance has been elaborated by Bertram H. Raven and Arie W. Kruglanski, "Conflict and Power," in Paul Swingle, ed., *The Structure of Conflict* (New York: Academic Press, 1970), pp. 69–109. For related material see the discussion of information dependence as a condition determining susceptibility to persuasion in Harold H. Kelley, "Attribution Theory in Social Psychology," in Daniel Levine, ed., *Nebraska Symposium on Motivation, 1967* (Lincoln, Nebr.: University of Nebraska Press, 1967), pp. 192–238.

25. See the description of attraction power in John R. P. French, Jr., and Bertram H. Raven, "The Bases of Social Power," in Dorwin Cartwright, ed., *Studies in Social Power* (Ann Arbor, Mich.: Institute for Social Research, 1959), pp. 150–67. See also the discussion of referent influence in Raven and Kruglanski, *op. cit.* For empirical evidence of the effectiveness of attraction power see R. S. Wilson, "Personality Patterns, Source Attractiveness and Conformity," *Journal of Personality*, XXVIII (1960), 186–99. For more on the reference group concept see Robert K. Merton and Alice S. Kitt, "Contributions to the Theory of Reference Group Behavior," in Robert K. Merton and Paul F. Lazersfeld, eds., *Continuities in Social Research: Studies in the Scope and Method of "the American Soldier"* (Glencoe, Ill.: Free Press, 1950), pp. 40–104.

26. See the discussion of legitimate power in French and Raven, *op. cit.*,

and Raven and Kruglanski, *op. cit.* For description of the effects of legitimacy in power relations see Bertram H. Raven and John R. P. French, Jr., "Legitimate Power, Coercive Power and Observability in Social Influence," *Sociometry*, XXI (1958), 83–97, and "Group Support, Legitimate Power and Social Influence," *Journal of Personality*, XXVI (1958), 400–9. An interesting inversion of position power especially pertinent to social work is the proposition that an individual tends to comply with the request of another who is, by virtue of a widely sanctioned norm, dependent upon him (the power of the sick over the healthy, the child over the adult). For elaboration of the power of the powerless, see Leonard Berkowitz and Louise R. Daniels, "Responsibility and Dependency," *Journal of Abnormal and Social Psychology*, LXVI (1963), 429–36; Louise R. Daniels and Leonard Berkowitz, "Liking and Response to Dependency Relationships," *Human Relations*, XVI (1963), 141–48; Thomas S. Szasz, *The Myth of Mental Illness: Foundations of a Theory of Personal Conduct* (New York: Hoeber-Harper, 1961); David Mechanic, "Sources of Power of Lower Participants in Complex Organizations," *Administrative Science Quarterly*, VII (1962), 349–64.

27. See description of expert power in French and Raven, *op. cit.*, and Raven and Kruglanski, *op. cit.* For related material see the discussion of abilities as exogenous determinants of rewards and costs in the theory of interaction outcomes by John W. Thibaut and Harold H. Kelley, *The Social Psychology of Groups* (New York: John Wiley, 1959).

28. See description of reward power and coercive power in French and Raven, *op. cit.*, and Raven and Kruglanski, *op. cit.* For empirical evidence of reward and punishment power see Sheila G. Zipf, "Resistance and Conformity under Reward and Punishment," *Journal of Abnormal and Social Psychology*, LXI (1960), 102–9. See also John R. P. French, Jr., H. William Morrison, and George Levinger, "Coercive Power and Forces Affecting Conformity," *Journal of Abnormal and Social Psychology*, LXI (1960), 93–101. Many theorists presume all of social influence to be a function of reward and punishment capability. For example, see the discussion of authority interactions in terms of operant conditioning principles, J. Stacy Adams and A. Kimball Romney, "A Functional Analysis of Authority," *Psychological Review*, LXVI (1959), 234–51, and "The Determinants of Authority Interactions," in Norman F. Washburne, ed., *Decisions, Values and Groups* (New York: Pergamon Press, 1962), II, 227–56. See also Thibaut and Kelley, *op. cit.*

29. See Raven and Kruglanski, *op. cit.*, and Raven and French, *op. cit.*

30. This proposition follows logically from the proposition preceding it. For details see Raven and Kruglanski, *op. cit.* An excellent discussion of surveillance in power relationships can be found in Thomas C.

Schelling, *The Strategy of Conflict* (New York: Oxford University Press, 1969).

31. See Raven and Kruglanski, *op. cit.*, and Raven and French, *op. cit.*

32. See L. Levine and J. Butler, "Lecture vs. Group Decision in Changing Behavior," *Journal of Applied Psychology*, XXXVI (1952), 29–33; John P. Dean and Alex Rosen, *A Manual of Intergroup Relations* (Chicago: University of Chicago Press, 1955); David Kipnis, "The Effects of Leadership Style and Leadership Power upon the Inducement of an Attitude Change," *Journal of Abnormal and Social Psychology*, LVII (1958), 173–80.

33. See the classic study using the autokinetic effect, Muzafer Sherif, "A Study of Some Social Factors in Perception," *Archives of Psychology*, Vol. XXVII, No. 187 (1935). See also Muzafer Sherif and O. J. Harvey, "A Study in Ego Functioning: Elimination of Stable Anchorages in Individual and Group Situations," *Sociometry*, XV (1952), 272–305; Richard S. Crutchfield, "Conformity and Character," *American Psychologist*, X (1955), 191–98; Muzafer Sherif and Carolyn Sherif, *An Outline of Social Psychology* (New York: Harper, 1956); Robert R. Blake, Harry Helson, and Jane S. Mouton, "The Generality of Conformity Behavior as a Function of Factual Anchorage, Difficulty of Task and Amount of Social Pressure," *Journal of Personality*, XXV (1957), 294–305; John Downing, "Cohesiveness, Perception and Values," *Human Relations*, XI (1958), 157–66.

34. Related studies include Leon Festinger, Stanley Schachter, and Kurt Back, *Social Pressures in Informal Groups: a Study of Human Factors in Housing* (New York: Harper, 1950); Harold H. Kelley and Martin M. Shapiro, "An Experiment on Conformity to Group Norms Where Conformity Is Detrimental to Group Achievement," *American Sociological Review*, XIX (1954), 667–68; John W. Thibaut and Lloyd H. Strickland, "Psychological Set and Social Conformity," *Journal of Personality*, XXV (1956), 115–29; J. S. Kidd, "Social Influence Phenomena in a Task-oriented Group Situation," *Journal of Abnormal and Social Psychology*, LVI (1958), 13–17; Ivan D. Steiner and Stanley C. Peters, "Conformity and the A-B-X Model," *Journal of Personality*, XXVI (1958), 229–42; Albert J. Lott and Bernice E. Lott, "Group Cohesiveness, Communication Level and Conformity," *Journal of Abnormal and Social Psychology*, LXII (1961), 408–12; Robert S. Wyer, Jr., "Effects of Incentive to Perform Well, Group Attraction and Group Acceptance on Conformity in a Judgmental Task," *Journal of Personality and Social Psychology*, IV (1966), 21–26.

35. Evidence to support the relationship between publicity and conformity was provided by Harold H. Kelley and E. H. Volkhart, "The Resistance to Change of Group Anchored Attitudes," *American Sociologi-*

cal Review, XVII (1952), 453–65; Carl I. Hoveland, Irving L. Janis, and Harold H. Kelley, *Communication and Persuasion: Psychological Studies of Opinion Change* (New Haven, Conn.: Yale University Press, 1953); Jane S. Mouton, Robert R. Blake, and Joseph Olmsted, "The Relationship between Frequency of Yielding and the Disclosure of Personal Identity," *Journal of Personality,* XXIV (1956), 339–47; Michael Argyle, "Social Pressure in Public and Private Situations," *Journal of Abnormal and Social Psychology,* LIV (1967), 172–75. For a discussion of the relationship between publicity and conformity as a function of attraction to the group see Leon Festinger and Elliot Aronson, "The Arousal and Reduction of Dissonance in Social Contexts," in Dorwin Cartwright and Alvin Zander, eds., *Group Dynamics: Research and Theory* (Evanston, Ill.: Row, Peterson, 1960), pp. 214–31.

36. Related studies include Edith B. Bennett, "Discussion, Decision, Commitment and Consensus in Group Decision," *Human Relations,* VIII (1955), 251–74; Abraham S. Luchins and Edith H. Luchins, "On Conformity with True and False Communications," *Journal of Social Psychology,* XLII (1955), 283–303; Harold H. Kelley and Christine L. Woodruff, "Members' Reactions to Apparent Group Approval of a Counternorm Communication," *Journal of Abnormal and Social Psychology,* LII (1956), 67–74.

37. For evidence when there is support for the individual's contrary opinion see Solomon E. Asch, "Effects of Group Pressure upon the Modification and Distortion of Judgment," in Harold S. Guetzkow, ed., *Groups, Leadership and Men* (Pittsburgh: Carnegie Institute Press, 1951), pp. 177–90; Mouton, Blake, and Olmsted, *op. cit.;* May Brodbeck, "The Role of Small Groups in Mediating the Effects of Propaganda," *Journal of Abnormal and Social Psychology,* LII (1956), 166–70. For evidence when there is lack of unanimity but no support see Marvin E. Shaw, Gerald H. Rothschild, and John F. Strickland, "Decision Processes in Communication Nets," *ibid.,* pp. 323–30.

38. See Eugene A. Weinstein and Paul Deutschberger, "Some Dimensions of Altercasting," *Sociometry,* XXVI (1963), 454–66. For further elaboration of the reciprocal nature of role-taking behavior see Theodore R. Sarbin, "Notes on the Transformation of Social Identity," in Leigh M. Roberts, Norman S. Greenfield and Milton H. Millers, eds., *Comprehensive Mental Health: the Challenge of Evaluation* (Madison, Wis.: University of Wisconsin Press, 1968), pp. 97–115. For an interesting perspective on reciprocal role-taking behavior in terms of "role bargaining" see William J. Goode, "A Theory of Role Strain," *American Sociological Review,* XXV (1960), 483–96.

39. Anthropological evidence for the occurrence of reciprocity in primitive societies has been reviewed by M. D. Sahlins, "On the Sociology

of Primitive Exchange," in *The Relevance of Models for Social Anthropology*, American Sociological Association Monographs, I (London: Tavistock Publications, 1965). For experimental evidence see Leonard Berkowitz, "Responsibility, Reciprocity and social Distance in Help-giving: an Experimental Investigation of English Social Class Differences," *Journal of Experimental and Social Psychology*, IV (1968), 46–63; John Schopler and V. D. Thompson, "Role of Attribution Processes in Mediating Amount of Reciprocity for a Favor," *Journal of Personality and Social Psychology*, X (1968), 243–50; Richard E. Gorenson and Leonard Berkowitz, "Reciprocity and Responsibility Reactions to Prior Help," *Journal of Personality and Social Psychology*, III (1966), 227–32. For an explanation of reciprocity as a social norm see Alvin W. Gouldner, "The Norm of Reciprocity: a Preliminary Statement," *American Sociological Review*, XXV (1960), 161–78.

40. For related material see Robert F. Bales, "The Equilibrium Problem in Small Groups," in Talcott Parsons, Robert F. Bales, and Edward A. Shils, *Working Papers in the Theory of Action* (New York: Free Press, 1953), pp. 111–61; Fred L. Strodtbeck, "The Family as a Three-Person Group," *American Sociological Review*, XIX (1954), 23–29; James G. March, "Influence Measurement in Experimental and Semiexperimental Groups," *Sociometry*, XIX (1956), 260–71; Bernard M. Bass, *et al.*, "Interacting Effects of Control, Motivation, Group Practice and Problem Difficulty on Attempted Leadership," *Journal of Abnormal and Social Psychology*, LVI (1958), 352–58; Henry W. Riecken, "The Effect of Talkativeness on Ability to Influence Group Solutions to Problems," *Sociometry*, XXI (1958), 309–21; John P. Kirscht, Thomas M. Lodahl, and Mason Haire, "Some Factors in the Selection of Leaders by Members of Small Groups," *Journal of Abnormal and Social Psychology*, LVIII (1969), 406–8.

41. For details see Steinzor, *op. cit.*; Fred L. Strodtbeck and L. Harmon Hook, "The Social Dimensions of a Twelve-Man Jury Table," *Sociometry*, XXIV (1961), 397–415. See especially the creative design and empirical confirmation for a more elaborate hypothesis in Lloyd T. Howells and Selwyn W. Becker, "Seating Arrangement and Leadership Emergence," *Journal of Abnormal and Social Psychology*, LXIV (1962), 148–50.

42. See Bernard M. Bass, "An Analysis of the Leaderless Group Discussion," *Journal of Applied Psychology*, XXXIII (1949), 527–33; Bernard M. Bass and Stanley Klubeck, "Effects of Seating Arrangement on Leaderless Group Discussion," *Journal of Abnormal and Social Psychology*, XLVII (1952), 724–27.

43. For details see Norman Gekoski, "Predicting Group Productivity," *Personnel Psychology*, V (1952), 281–92; Leonard Berkowitz, "Sharing Leadership in Small Decision-making Groups," *Journal of Abnormal and*

Social Psychology, XLVIII (1953), 231–38; Robert L. Kahn and Daniel Katz, "Leadership Practices in Relation to Productivity and Morale," in Dorwin Cartwright and Alvin Zander, eds., *op. cit.*, pp. 612–28.

44. For details see Stuart Adams, "Status Congruity as a Variable in Small Group Performance," *Social Forces*, XXXII (1953), 16–22; Christof Heinicke and Robert F. Bales, "Developmental Trends in the Structure of Small Groups," *Sociometry*, XVI (1953), 7–38; Robert F. Bales and Phillip E. Slater, "Role Differentiation in Small Decision-making Groups," in Talcott Parsons *et al., The Family, Socialization and Interaction Processes* (New York: Free Press, 1955), pp. 259–306; Clovis Shepherd and Irving R. Weschler, "The Relation between Three Interpersonal Variables and Communication Effectiveness: a Pilot Study," *Sociometry*, XVIII (1955), 103–10; D. K. Wheeler, "Notes on 'Role Differentiation in Small Decision-making Groups,'" *Sociometry*, XX (1957), 145–51; Robert F. Bales and Phillip E. Slater, "Notes on 'Role Differentiation in Small Decision-making Groups': Reply to Dr. Wheeler," *ibid.*, pp. 152–55.

45. See Leon Festinger and John Thibaut, "Interpersonal Communication in Small Groups," *Journal of Abnormal and Social Psychology*, XLVI (1951), 92–99; Stanley Schachter, "Deviation, Rejection and Communication," *ibid.*, pp. 190–207.

46. See the discussion of idiosyncracy credit in Edwin P. Hollander, "Conformity, Status and Idiosyncracy Credit," *Psychological Review*, LXV (1958), 117–27.

47. For evidence with an intellectual group task see Jack R. Gibb, "The Effects of Group Size and Threat Reduction upon Creativity in a Problem-solving Situation," *American Psychologist*, VI (1951), 324. See also the discussion of Moede's 1927 study in which a similar effect was noted with a physical task in A. Paul Hare, *Handbook of Small Group Research* (New York: Free Press, 1962), pp. 388–89.

48. Related theory and research include Paul J. Hoffman, Leon Festinger, and Douglas Lawrence, "Tendencies toward Group Comparability in Competitive Bargaining," *Human Relations*, VII (1954), 141–59; W. Edgar Vinacke and Abe Arkoff, "Experimental Study of Coalitions in the Triad," *American Sociological Review*, XXII (1957), 406–15; Theodore Caplow, "Further Development of a Theory of Coalitions in the Triad." *American Journal of Sociology*, LXIV (1959), 488–93; Marilyn V. Chaney and W. Edgar Vinacke, "Achievement and Nurturance in Triads Varying in Power Distribution," *Journal of Abnormal and Social Psychology*, LX (1960), 175–81; Harold H. Kelley and A. John Arrowood, "Coalitions in the Triad: Critique and Experiment," *Sociometry*, XXIII (1960), 231–44.

49. For an explanation in terms of parity and investment-return ratios

see William A. Gamson, "A Theory of Coalition Formation" and "An Experimental Test of a Theory of Coalition Formation," *American Sociological Review*, XXVI (1961), 373–82, 565–73.

50. See Muzafer Sherif, B. J. White, and O. J. Harvey, "Status in Experimentally Produced Groups," *American Journal of Sociology*, LX (1955), 370–79.

51. For details see Muzafer Sherif, "A Preliminary Study of Intergroup Relations," in John H. Rohrer and Muzafer Sherif, eds., *Social Psychology at the Crossroads: University of Oklahoma Lectures in Social Psychology* (New York: Harper, 1951), pp. 388–424; Muzafer Sherif and Carolyn W. Sherif, *Groups in Harmony and Tension* (New York: Harper, 1953).

52. For empirical evidence see Elliott Aronson and Judson Mills, "The Effect of Severity of Initiation on Liking for a Group," *Journal of Abnormal and Social Psychology*, XLIX (1959), 177–81. For an explanation in terms of cognitive dissonance reduction see Festinger and Aronson, *op. cit.*

53. See Albert Mehrabian, "Some Referents and Measures on Nonverbal Behavior," *Behavior Research Method and Instruction*, I (1969), 203–7; Albert Mehrabian, "Significance of Posture and Position in the Communication of Status Relationships," *Psychological Bulletin*, LXXI (1969), 359–72.

54. See Pavel Machotka, "Body Movements as Communication," *Dialogues, Behavioral Science Research*, II (1965), 33–65.

55. See William T. James, "A Study of the Expression of Bodily Posture," *Journal of General Psychology*, VII (1932), 403–37; Michael N. Reece and Robert N. Whitman, "Expressive Movements and Verbal Reinforcement," *Journal of Abnormal and Social Psychology*, LXIV (1962), 204–36; Mehrabian, "Significance of Posture and Position in the Communication of Status Relationships."

56. For an anthropological perspective see Edward T. Hall, *The Silent Language* (New York: Fawcett, 1959); Edward T. Hall, "A System for the Notation of Proxemic Behavior," *American Anthropologist*, LXV (1963), 1003–26; Edward T. Hall, *The Hidden Dimension* (New York: Doubleday, 1966); Harold Garfinkle, "Studies of the Routine Grounds of Everyday Activities," *Social Problems*, XI (1964), 225–50; Kenneth B. Little, "Personal Space," *Journal of Experimental Social Psychology*, I (1965), 237–47; N. J. Felipe and Robert Sommer, "Invasions of Personal Space," *Social Problems*, XIV (1966), 206–14. For an interesting study of the subjective meaning of distance behavior using a semantic differential see Paul Goldring, "Role of Distance and Posture in the Evaluation of Interactions," *Proceedings of the 75th Annual Convention of the American Psychological Association* (1967), II, 243–44.

57. Evidence can be found in Phoebe C. Ellsworth and J. Merril Carlsmith, "Effects of Eye Contact and Verbal Content on Affective Response to a Dyadic Interaction," *Journal of Personality and Social Psychology*, X (1968), 15–20; Paul Ekman and Wallace V. Friesen, "Nonverbal Leakage and Clues to Deception," *Psychiatry*, XXXII (1969), 88–106.

58. See John A. Starkweather, "Vocal Communication of Personality and Human Feelings," *Journal of Communications*, II (1961), 63–72.

59. See Mehrabian, "Some Referents and Measures on Nonverbal Behavior."

60. See Reece and Whitman, *op. cit.;* Allen T. Dittmann, Morris B. Parloff, and Donald S. Boomer, "Facial and Bodily Expression: a Study of Receptivity of Emotional Cues," *Psychiatry*, XXVIII (1965), 239–44; Ekman and Friesen, *op. cit.*

61. Briar and Miller, *op. cit.*

CHAPTER 13: TOWARD EFFECTIVE PRACTICE

1. Ronald Gross and Paul Osterman, eds., *The New Professionals* (New York: Simon and Schuster, 1972), p. 11.

2. Scott Briar, "The Current Crisis in Social Casework," in *Social Work Practice, 1967* (New York: Columbia University Press, 1967), pp. 19–33; Joel Fischer, "Is Casework Effective? A Review," *Social Work*, XVIII. No. 1 (1973), 5–20.

3. Scott Briar, "Effective Social Work Intervention in Direct Practice: Implications for Education," in Scott Briar *et al., Facing the Challenge: Plenary Session Papers from the 19th Annual Program Meeting* (New York: Council on Social Work Education, 1973) pp. 17–30.

4. Robert F. Mager, *Preparing Instructional Objectives* (Belmont, Calif.: Fearon, 1962), p. vii; emphasis added.

Index